The Book of the Cave of Treasures

Translated by

E. A. Wallis Budge

ISBN: 978-1-63923-486-8

Printed: November 2022

Cover Art By: Amit Paul

Published and Distributed By:
Lushena Books
607 Country Club Drive, Unit E
Bensenville, IL 60106
www.lushenabks.com

ISBN: 978-1-63923-486-8

The Book of the Cave of Treasures

A History of the Patriarchs and the Kings, their Successors from the Creation to the Crucifixion of Christ

Translated by

E. A. Wallis Budge

PUBLISHER'S PREFACE

About the Book

"The Cave of Treasures, sometimes referred to simply as The Treasure, is a book of the New Testament apocrypha. This text is attributed to Ephrem Syrus, who was born at Nisibis soon after A.D. 306 and died in 373, but it is now generally believed that the form in which we now have it is not older than the 6th century."

CONTENTS

PREFACE

THE present volume contains a complete translation of the Syriac text of the compendious history of the world from the Creation to the Crucifixion of our Lord, which is commonly known as "Me`ârath Gazzê," or the "Cave of Treasures." In the Syriac title the composition of the work is attributed to Ap[h]rêm Suryâyâ, i.e. Ephrem Syrus, or Ephraim the Syrian, who was born at Nisibis (?) soon after A.D. 306 and died in 373, but it is now generally believed that the form in which we now have it is not older than the VIth century. An edition of the Syriac text, and an Arabic version of it, together with a German translation, were published by Bezold (Die Schatzhöhle, Munich, 1883-86), but this work is scarce and is little known in England. The German translation was made from an eclectic text constructed from at least three manuscripts, which varied in age and accuracy and general literary value. The translation given in the following pages has been p. xii made from the best, in my opinion, of all the known manuscripts, namely British Museum MS. Add. 25875. (See Wright, Catalogue, vol. iii, page 1064.) This MS. contains twelve complete works, all of which were written, in a fine Nestorian hand, by the priest Homô, the son of the priest Daniel, a native of Al-Kôsh, a very ancient town which lies about 20 miles north of Môsul (Nineveh), in the year of the Greeks 2020, i.e. A.D. 1709. It was written at the expense of the priest Joseph, the son of Hormizd, a native of Hordaphne, in the district of ´Amediâ, for the church of the Blessed Virgin Mary in that place. When I read through the manuscript in 1885, whilst preparing my edition of the "Book of the Bee," I was convinced that Homô, the scribe, was a very learned man, and the marginal notes which he added to his copy showed that he was at once a capable and an understanding editor of Syriac texts. When the printed edition of the Syriac text of the "Cave of Treasures" appeared in 1886, I was surprised to find that Homô's text had not been made the foundation of the work. Whilst I was in Al-Kôsh in 1890-91 collecting manuscripts for the British Museum, I found there some of Homô's descendants, and of these one or two were professional scribes. They possessed a few ancient Syriac manuscripts, and from one of them I had copies made of the p. xiii "Cave of Treasures" and the "Book of the Bee." On my return to England I collated the copy of the former work with the British Museum Codex, and found that the text only varied in a few minor points. There are a few mistakes in the British Museum MS., and in one or two places a few words are omitted, but as a whole it contains the text of the "Cave of Treasures" in as perfect form as ever we are likely to get it; and therefore I have made the translation printed herein from it.

A text of this kind might be annotated to almost any extent, but I have limited my notes to pointing out parallels in the "Book of Jubilees," the "Book of Adam and Eve," the "Book of the Bee," and other cognate works. These are printed within square brackets immediately following the passages in the "Cave of Treasures" which they illustrate. In the short Bibliography which follows the translation will be found the names of a number of books and of editions of texts which those who are interested in the literary history of the "Cave of Treasures" will find necessary for useful work. I have also added a translation of the "Testament of Adam," a popular apocryphal work which is based upon the Syriac "Cave of Treasures," and upon legends derived from books of a similar, and perhaps allied, character.

The ancient tradition which asserts that the "Cave of Treasures" was written in the IVth century of our Era, is supported by the general contents of the work. These reproduce Ephraim's quaint and sometimes fanciful methods of exegesis and his hatred of the Jews, and supply many examples of his methods in religious argument with which we are familiar from his other writings. We may notice, too, his pride in the antiquity of the Syriac language. That it was written in Mesopotamia by a Syrian, there is no doubt, and if we reject Ephraim as its author, we are bound to admit that the author, or perhaps later editor, belonged to the school of Ephraim. Whichever view be taken is immaterial. For the book certainly contains a mass of historical information which can only have been derived from pre-Christian Hebrew works, or from post-Christian chronologies and histories written in Greek. The writers of such Greek works derived some of their information at first or second hand, from documents originally written in cuneiform. Of the general historical character of the "Cave of Treasures" there is no doubt, and it is this fact which gives it such importance for the history of the Hebrew Patriarchs, and for early Christian History, and the Christian Faith. This view was maintained by the eminent scholars Dillmann, Nöldeke, p. xv Sachau, Wright, Bezold and others during the last century, and it was firmly held by Christians in Mesopotamia, Syria,

Palestine, Egypt, Nubia and Abyssinia for the fourteen centuries preceding.

On the historical facts which form the framework of the "Cave of Trea-sures," the pious author, or editor, grafted a whole series of legends, many of which deserve the descriptions of "idle stories" and "vain fables" which have been applied to them by Assemânî and the older European theolo-gians. The reader having perused them will readily understand that such legends, containing as they do garbled history facts and anachronisms, are neither accepted nor endorsed by any member of the Committee of the Religious Tract Society or by myself. These legends were inserted with the view of making the "Cave of Treasures" a sort of religious "wonder-book" which would appeal to the vivid and credulous imaginations of Christian natives in almost every country of the Near East; and religious "wonder-books" were intended by their authors and editors to amuse as well as to instruct. The "Cave of Treasures" possesses an apocryphal character it is true, but the support which its contents give to the Christian Faith, and the light which the historical portions of it throw on early Christian History, entitle it to a very high place among the apocryphal Books of the Old and p. xvi the New Testament. These facts have induced the Committee of the Religious Tract Society to order the publication of this the first English translation of the "Cave of Treasures."

My thanks are due to the Trustees of the British Museum for permission to publish a photographic reproduction of the cylinder of Cyrus and photo-graphs of Ethiopic and Syriac MSS.; to Sir Frederick Kenyon, K.C.B., and the late Dr. Byron Gordon for permission to copy the photographs made by Mr. C. L. Woolley, M.A., for the Joint Expedition, of the objects found at "Ur of the Chaldees"; to the Art Editor of The Times for a copy of the photograph of "Abraham's Street" at Ur; to Mr. C. L. Woolley for the use of his notes and descriptions of the antiquities found at Ur; to the Rev. C. H. Irwin, D.D., General Editor of the Religious Tract Society, for his friendly criticisms, and to Mr. H. R. Brabrook for his practical suggestions.

E. A. WALLIS BUDGE

48, Bloomsbury Street,
  Bedford Square, London, W.C. 1.
    July 30, 1927.

INTRODUCTION

THE SOURCES OF THE "CAVE OF TREASURES" AND ITS CONTENTS

I N the centuries immediately preceding the Christian Era certain professional Jewish scribes composed a number of works which may well be described as "historical romances," and which were based on the histories of the patriarchs and others as found in the four main divisions of the text of the Hebrew Bible. There is little doubt that most of these works were written either in Hebrew or in the Palestinian vernacular of the period. One of the oldest of such works appears to be the "Book of Jubilees" (see page 3), (also called the "Lesser Genesis" and the "Apocalypse of Moses"), which derives its name from the fact that the periods of time described in it are Jubilees, i.e. each period contains forty-nine years. It is more or less a Commentary on the Book of Genesis. That a version of this book existed in Greek is proved by the quotations given by Epiphanius, Bishop of Salamis in Cyprus (born about A.D. 320, and died in 403 or 404), in his work on "Heresies" (chapter xxxix). The author claimed boldly that his work contains the revelations which were made to Moses by the command of God by the Archangel Michael, who is frequently described as the "Angel of the Face," The book is not wholly original, for it contains narratives and traditions derived from the works of earlier writers; and some of the legends appear to have been taken from early Babylonian sources. The Hebrew, or Aramean, original is lost, and the complete work is only found in Ethiopic, in which language it is known as "Kûfâlê," or "Sections." The Ethiopic translation was made from Greek.

Another pre-Christian work, also written by a Jew, is the "Book of Enoch," which exists now in a more or less complete form, only in an Ethiopic translation, which was made from the Greek. This work is quoted by St. Jude (vv. 14, 15), and there is little doubt that for some three or four centuries its authority, both among the Jews and the Christians of the first and second centuries of our Era, was very great. Whether the "Book of Enoch," as made known to us by the Ethiopic version, truly represents the original Hebrew work is fairly open to doubt; in fact, it seems certain that it does not. It contains a series of fragments or parts of works, of somewhat similar character, which has been strung together, and then added to by writers of different schools of religious thought at different periods. In some parts of it traces have been found of beliefs which are neither Jewish nor Christian. (See page 5.)

From time to time during the early centuries of the Christian Era apocryphal works dealing with our Lord and His Apostles and disciples appeared, and, though they were written by Christians, they contained many legends and traditions which their authors borrowed from the works of earlier Jewish and Christian writers. Such works were very popular among the Christian communities of Egypt and Syria, for the thirst for information about our Lord and His life and works, and the adventures and successes of the Apostles in Africa, Western Asia, India and other countries was very great. Side by side with this apocryphal literature there appeared works in Egypt and Syria which dealt with Old Testament History and endeavoured to explain its difficulties. But though Patriarch and Bishop and Priest read the Scriptures and the commentaries on them to the people, and instructed their congregations orally on every possible occasion, there was much in the ancient Jewish Religion, out of which many of the aspects of the Christian Religion had developed, which the laity did not understand. On the one hand, the unlettered Christian folk heard the Jews denouncing Christ and His followers, and on the other, their teachers taught them that Christ was a descendant of King David and Abraham, and that the great and essential truths and mysteries of the Christian Religion were foreshadowed by events which had taken place in the lives of the Jewish patriarchs.

Some of the Fathers of the Church in the Vth and VIth centuries wrote sermons and dissertations on the Birth of our Lord, and His Baptism, Temptation, Passion and Death and Resurrection, and proved by quotations from the Prophets that the son of the Virgin Mary was indeed the Messiah and the Saviour of the world. But copies of these works were not multiplied for the use of their congregations, most of the members of which were unlettered folk, and the influence of all written discourses was much circumscribed in consequence. The great monastic institutions possessed copies of the Old and New Testaments written in Greek and Syriac, but these were not available for study by the laity in general, and it is probable that only well-to-do people could afford to have copies of the Books of the Bible made for their private use. Thus the circumstances of the time made it necessary that the Fathers of the Church, or some of the learned scribes, should compile comprehensive works on the history of God's dealings with man as described in the Old Testament, and show the true relationship of the Christian Religion to the Religion of the Hebrew Patriarchs and the to kings of Israel and Judah. There is little doubt that many such works were written, and that their authors based their histories on the writings of their predecessors, and that Christian writers borrowed largely from the Hebrew "Book of Enoch" and the "Book of Jubilees," as well as the Histories and Chronicles which were then extant in Greek. Some of the latter works, i.e. those in Greek, were written by men who had access to information which was derived from Babylonian and Assyrian histories written in cuneiform, and, thanks to the labours of Assyriologists, the statements based on such information can, in many cases, be checked and verified. Further reference to this point will be made later on.

The oldest of the Christian works on the history of God's dealing with man from Adam to Christ is probably the "Book of Adam and Eve" (see page 9), which, in its original form, was written sometime in the Vth or VIth century of our Era; its author is unknown. As there is no doubt whatever that the writer of the "Cave of Treasures" borrowed largely from the "Book of Adam and Eve," or from the same source from which its writer derived his information, it is necessary to give here a brief description of the object and contents of this work.

The oldest manuscript of the "Book of Adam and Eve" known to us is in Arabic and is not older than the XIth century. But many of the legends and traditions found in it are identical in form and expression with those found in the "Annals" of Sa`îd bin al-Batrîk, or Eutychius, Patriarch of Alexandria (A.D. 933-939), and in the "Eight Books of Mysteries" written by Clement about A.D. 750, and in the "Cave of Treasures," which is now generally thought to have been written, or perhaps re-edited, in the VIth century. The Arabic version of the "Book of Adam and Eve" contains two main sections. The first contains a History of the Creation, which claims to be a translation of the "Hexemeron" of Epiphanius, Bishop in Cyprus. In it are given an account of the work of the six days of Creation, the Vision of Gregory concerning the Fall of Satan, a description of the Four Heavens, the Creation of Man, the temptation of Eve, and the expulsion of Adam and Eve from Paradise. The title, "Book of the Aksîmâris," would lead one to suppose that the whole work was devoted to the Creation, but it is not, for the second Section contains "The History of the departure of Adam and Eve from Paradise, and their arrival in the Cave of Treasures by the command of God."

The writer of the "Book of Adam and Eve" meant the two sections to form a complete work. The first shows how Adam fell, and the second tells us how God fulfilled the promise which He made to Adam more than once, that after five and a half weeks, i.e. 5,500 years, He would send a Redeemer into the world who would save both Adam and his descendants from the destruction which his sin in Paradise had incurred, The writer of the book gives the History of Adam and Eve in full, adding as he progresses in his work the various legends and traditions which he found in the works of his predecessors. This plan he follows until he comes to the Flood, and on to the time of Melchisedek; but, having settled this king in Salem, the rest of his work becomes a bald recital of genealogies, only rarely interspersed with explanations and generalizations. Whether he was a Jacobite or Nestorian there is nothing to show in his work, and it seems that he hated the Jews not because of their religion, but because they had crucified Christ, and had also, in his opinion, promulgated a false genealogy of Joseph and the Virgin Mary.

Of the author of the "Book of Adam and Eve" nothing is known. Some have thought that he was a pious and orthodox Egyptian, who wrote in Coptic and derived the legends and traditions which he incorporated in his book from documents written in Greek or Syriac or from native works of the Coptic Church. Dr. W. Meyer discovered and published (in the Abhandlungen of the Bavarian Academy, Bd. XIV, III Abth.) two versions of the Life of Adam and Eve, one in Greek and the other in Latin. The Greek version is called the Ἀποκάλυψις Ἀδάμ {Greek: ʿApokálupsis ʿAdàm}. (Apocalypse of Adam), and the Latin "Vita Adae et Evae." Their contents differ materially, and neither version can be regarded as derived from the "Book of Adam and Eve" described above. Like the "Book of Jubilees" and the "Book of Enoch," the "Book of Adam and Eve" exists in a complete form only in Ethiopic, where it is called "GADLA ʿADÂM WA HÊWÂN," i.e. "The Fight of Adam and Eve [against Satan]." The best known text is given in a manuscript in the British Museum (Oriental No. 751. See Wright, Catalogue No. cccxx, page 213), which was written in the reign of Bakâffâ, king of Abyssinia, 1721-1730. It was one of the chief authorities used by Trumpp in the preparation of his edition of the Ethiopic text which appeared at Munich in 1880. The forms of several of the Biblical names indicate that the Ethiopic translation was made from Arabic. Translations of the complete book have been made by Dillmann, Das Christliche Adambuch, Göttingen, 1853, and Malan, The Book of Adam and Eve, London, 1882.

The discovery of the existence of the Book called the "Cave of Treasures" we owe to Assemânî, the famous author of the Catalogues of Oriental Manuscripts in the Vatican Library, which he printed in Bibliotheca Orientalis in four thick volumes folio. In Vol. ii. page 498 he describes a Syriac manuscript containing a series of apocryphal works, and among them is one the title of which he translates by "Spelunca Thesaurorum." He read the MS. carefully and saw that it contained the history of a period of 5,500 years, i.e. from the creation of Adam to the birth of Christ, and that it was a historical chronicle based upon the Scriptures. He says that fables are found in it everywhere, and especially in that part of it which treats of the antediluvian Patriarchs, and the genealogy of Christ and His Mother. He mentions that the Patriarch Eutychius also describes a cave of treasures in which gold, frankincense, and myrrh were laid up, and refers to the "portentosa feminarum nomina," who were the ancestresses of Christ. No attempt was made to publish the Syriac text; in fact, little attention was paid to it until Dillmann began to study the " Book of Adam and Eve" in connection with it, and then he showed in Ewald's Jahrbüchern (Bd. V. 1853) that the contents of whole sections of the "Book of the Cave of Treasures" in Syriac and the "Book of Adam and Eve" in Ethiopic were identical. And soon after this Dillmann and others noticed that an Arabic MS. in the Vatican (No. XXXIX; see Assemânî, Bibl. Orient. i. page 281) contained a version of the "Cave of Treasures," which had clearly been made from the Syriac. In 1883 Bezold published a translation of the Syriac text of the "Cave of Treasures" made from three manuscripts (Die Schatzhöhle, Leipzig, 1883), and five years later published the Syriac text of it, accompanied by the text of the Arabic version.

In 1885 I was engaged in preparing an edition, of the Syriac text of the "DEBHÛRÎTHÂ," i.e. the "Bee," a "Book of Gleanings" composed by the Nestorian Bishop Solomon of Basra (i.e. al-Basrah) about A.D. 1222. Whilst making the English translation of this work I found that the "Bee" contained many of the legends and traditions which appeared in the "Cave of Treasures," and to show how greatly the Nestorian Bishop Solomon had borrowed from the work of the Jacobite author of the "Cave of Treasures" in the earlier part of his work, I printed several lengthy extracts from the Syriac from the fine manuscript in the British Museum, together with English translations (see The Book of the Bee, the Syrian Text with an English translation, Oxford, 1886; Anecdota Oxoniensia, Semitic Series, Vol. I, Part II), and these were thought to emphasize the general importance of the "Cave of Treasures."

The author of the Book which is commonly known as the "Cave of Treasures" called his work "The Book of the order of the succession of Generations (or Families)," the Families being those of the Patriarchs and Kings of Israel and Judah; and his chief object was to show how Christ was descended from Adam. He did not accept the genealogical tables which were commonly in use among his unlearned fellow-Christians, because he was convinced that all the ancient tables of genealogies which the Jews had possessed were destroyed by fire by the captain of Nebuchadnezzar's army immediately after the capture of Jerusalem by the Babylonians. The Jews promptly constructed new tables of genealogies, which both Christians and Arabs regarded as fictitious. The Arabs were as deeply interested in the matter as the Christians, for they were descended from Abraham, and the genealogy of the descendants of Hagar and Ishmael was of the greatest importance in their sight, and it is due to their earnest desire to possess correct genealogical tables of their ancestors that we owe the Arabic translations of the "Cave of Treasures." The Nubians and Egyptians were also interested in such matters, for the former were the descendants of Kûsh, and the latter the descendants of Mizraim, and Ham was the great ancestor of both these nations. And it is clear that Syrians, Arabs, Egyptians and Ethiopians regarded the "Cave of Treasures" as an authoritative work on their respective pedigrees.

In the title "Cave of Treasures" which was given to the "Book of the order of the succession of Generations" there is probably a double allusion, namely, to the Book as the storehouse of literary treasures, and to the famous Cave in which Adam and Eve were made to dwell by God after their expulsion from Paradise, and which by reason of the gold, and frankincense, and myrrh that was laid up in it, is commonly called "The Cave of Treasures" (in Syriac "Me`ârath Gazzê," in Arabic "Ma`ârah al-Kanûz," and in Ethiopic "Ba`âta Mazâgebet"). Now the Syriac work, though called the "Cave of Treasures," tells us very little about the real Cave, which was situated in the side of a mountain below Paradise, and nothing about the manner of life which Adam and Eve lived in it. But in the "Book of Adam and Eve" the whole of the first main section is devoted to the latter subject, and from this the following notes are taken:--

When Adam and Eve left Paradise they went into a strange land, and were terrified at the stones and sand which they saw before them, and became like dead folk. Then God sent His Word to them, and He told them that after five and a half weeks, i.e. 5,500 years, He would come in the flesh and save man. He had already made them this promise in Paradise, when they stood by the tree of forbidden fruit. The Cave of Treasures was a dark and gloomy place, and over it hung a huge rock, and when Adam and Eve entered it they were sorely troubled. God sent the birds, and beasts, and reptiles to Adam, and ordered them to be friendly to him and his descendants, and every kind of creature came to him except the serpent. In their grief Adam and Eve tried to drown themselves, but an angel was sent to drag them out of the water which flowed from the roots of the Tree of Life, and the Word restored them to life. Whilst they were living there God taught them how to wash their bodies, and told them what to eat and drink, and made known to them the use of wheat,[1] and showed them how to clothe themselves with the skins of beasts, and other essentials of civilization. There was no night in Paradise, and when the sun set and night fell on Adam his terror was great; at length God told him that the night was made for the beasts and himself to rest in, and explained to him the divisions of time, years, months, days, etc.

During the period of the abode of Adam and Eve in the Cave, Satan came and tempted them fourteen times, but whenever God saw that they were in danger of life or limb through the devilish wiles of the Evil One, He sent an angel to deliver them and put the Devil to flight. Adam suffered sorely from the heat of the sun, which caused him to fall down a precipice, and wound himself so severely that his blood flowed out of his body on to the ground. When God raised him up, he took stones, and builded an altar. And having wiped up his blood with leaves, and collected the dust which was saturated with blood, he offered both the leaves and the dust as an offering to God, Who accepted this, Adam's first offering, and sent a fire to consume it. As Adam shed his blood, and died through his wounds--which God healed--so also did the Word shed His blood and suffer death. Thus the blood-offering originated with Adam.

When God saw that Adam was terrified by the darkness of the night, He sent Michael into Judea, and told him to bring back tablets of gold, and when they arrived God set them in the Cave to lighten the darkness of the night therein. And God sent Gabriel into Paradise to fetch incense, and Raphael to bring myrrh from the same place, and these symbolic substances being placed in the Cave, Adam was comforted. Because the Cave contained these precious substances, it was called the "Cave of Treasures." A little later God permitted figs to be brought to Adam from Paradise, and taught Adam and Eve to cook food on the fire which was brought to them out of the hand of the fiery angel who stood at the entrance to Paradise holding a fiery sword in his hand. As Adam could not obtain a supply of blood to maintain the blood-offering, he laid upon the altar outside the Cave an offering made of wheat, presumably a loaf or cake baked in hot ashes, and God accepted it and sent a fire to consume it, the Holy Ghost being present. And God said that He would, when He came down upon the earth, make it to be His flesh, which was to be offered up continually upon an altar for forgiveness and mercy. And an angel took a part of the offering with a pair of fire-tongs, and administered it to Adam and Eve. Thereupon Adam established the custom of offering the wheat-offering thrice in the week, viz. on the first, fourth, and sixth days of the week.

After Adam had lived two hundred and twenty-three days in the Cave, God sent His angels to tell him to take Eve to wife, and to give the gold plates in the Cave to Eve as a betrothal gift. Adam obeyed the divine command, and in due course Eve bore him twins, Cain and his sister Lûwâ, in a cave under the huge rock which Satan once hurled at Adam, wishing to kill him. Later, Eve again brought forth twins, Abel and his sister, 'Aklemyâ. The remainder of the first section of the "Book of Adam and Eve" records the story of the murder of Abel by Cain, and tells how the earth rejected thrice Abel's body which Cain tried to bury in it.

It is now generally thought that the Syriac work which is called the "Cave of Treasures" was written in the VIth century of our Era, and in the absence of any evidence to the contrary this view may be accepted. In the title it is attributed to Ephraim the Syrian, and this indicates that the Syrians themselves were prepared to believe that it was written early in the IVth century, for this great writer died A.D. 373. Even if this attribution be wrong, it is important as suggesting that, if not written by Ephrem himself, one of his disciples, or some member of his school, may have been the author of the book.

Where the writer lived is not known, but it is most probable that it was written in Edessa or Nisibis; in any case, it must have been written in Mesopotamia, and the writer was certainly a Syrian Jacobite who was proud of his native language. Thus, having spoken of the migration of his people to Shinar, he says, "They all sat down there, and from Adam until the present time they were all of one speech and one language. They all speak this language, that is to say, 'Suryâyâ' (Syriac), which is 'Ârâmâyâ'

(Aramean), and this language is the king of all languages. Now, ancient writers have erred in that they said that Hebrew was the first [language], and in this matter they have mingled an ignorant mistake in their writing. For all the languages that are in the world are derived from Syriac, and all the languages in books are mingled with it" (page 132). And in another place he says that Pilate did right in writing the inscription which was placed on the Cross in Greek, Latin, and Hebrew only, and that he did not add a translation of it in Syriac because no Syrian played any part in the crucifixion of our Lord (page 230). And he goes on to say that the Syrians had no hand in shedding the blood of Christ, because Abhgar, King of Edessa, wanted to go and take Jerusalem, and slay the Jews who had crucified Him.[2] And, as Bezold pointed out, the name of Noah's wife, Haikal-bath-Nâmôs, and the names of several other women, appear to be of Syrian origin.

The writer's boast that Syriac is the oldest of all languages is probably not strictly true, but there is no doubt, in my opinion, that it is one of the oldest of the northern Semitic dialects. This is proved by the inscriptions on the Cappadocian tablets which have been acquired during the last few years by the British Museum. These tablets were written in connection with the commercial transactions of a settlement of Semitic traders, who flourished in the region of Caesarea about 2400 B.C. They conducted a brisk trade with Assyria in metals and textile fabrics, the latter coming from the Bulgar Dagh, and the former from the great cotton-growing districts which lay along the Khâbûr. The cuneiform texts of a large number of these commercial documents and letters have been published by Sidney Smith (Cuneiform Texts from Cappadocian Tablets, London, 1921 and following years), and in Part I he has given (pages 6 and 7) a long list of words used in connection with the weaving industry, which can be paralleled in Syriac by words of precisely the same roots. And this will probably be found to apply to the other objects of daily life, for the Syriac writers of the early centuries of the Christian Era knew of hundreds of words used in the affairs and business of daily life which they had no opportunity to use when writing the lives of saints, commentaries on the Scriptures, and works of a purely religious character.

Of the subsequent history of the Syriac Cave of Treasures very little is known. The knowledge of parts of it made its way into Armenia soon after the book was written, and more than one translation of it was made into Arabic, probably in the VIIth and VIIIth centuries. In connection with the

Arabic translations it must be noted that they all end with the account of the cruelties perpetrated by Archelaus and Sâlûm after the death of Herod. (See Bezold's text, page 247.) The last paragraph of the Arabic text mentions the twelve Apostles who went about with Christ, and refers to His baptisim by John the Baptist, and says that He lived on the earth thirty-three years, and then ascended into heaven. Thus for the last twenty-six pages of the Syriac text there is no equivalent in the Arabic version or translation. And the same is substantially true for the Ethiopic text of the "Book of Adam and Eve" The section of the Syriac for which there is no rendering in Arabic or Ethiopic contains a series of statements addressed by the author to his "brother Nemesius." It is possible that these have been added to the work by a later writer, but I do not think so. As they do not deal with matters of genealogy, and do treat almost exclusively of the life of Christ and His crucifixion, it is probable that they failed to interest the Arab translator, and he left them untranslated. It may be, however, that the complete Arabic translation has not come down to us.

Of the "brother Nemesius" mentioned above we know nothing. Judging by the form in which the author of the "Cave of Treasures" put his information before him, we might conclude that he was a friend whom he was specially anxious to convince of the truth of what he was going to write. Or, he may have been an opponent with whom he was conducting an argument on the birth, and life, and crucifixion of our Lord, and whom he was anxious to convert. Among the ancient celebrities who bore the name of Nemesius, the best known are Nemesius, the governor of Cappadocia, and friend of Gregory Nazianzen, Bishop of Sasima and Constantinople, and Nemesius, the Bishop of Emesa; both flourished in the latter half of the IVth century. The former was a pagan, but he was favourably disposed towards Christianity; whether Gregory succeeded in converting him is not known. It is clear from the "Cave of Treasures" that the Nemesius addressed by its author was a person of great importance, and some have thought that the governor of Cappadocia is the person referred to. He can hardly have been the Bishop of Emesa, who was, of course, a believing Christian. If the Nemesius mentioned was the governor of Cappadocia, it would support the view taken by the Syrians that the "Cave of Treasures" in its original form dates from the time of Ephrem the Syrian, i.e. the IVth century.

That the Syriac "Cave of Treasures" was known and used by Solomon, Bishop of Perâth Maishân (Al-Basrah) in 1222 is proved by the earlier chapters of his work the "Book of the Bee." He excerpted from it many of the legends of the early Patriarchs, although his object was not to write a table of genealogical succession, but a full history of the Christian Dispensation according to the views of the Nestorians. It is interesting to note that we owe the best manuscript of the "Cave of Treasures" which we have to the Nestorians, for Brit. Mus. MS. Add. 25875, was written by a Nestorian scribe in the Nestorian village of Alkôsh, and was bound up by him in a volume which included a copy of the "Book of the Bee," whose author, Solomon, was the Nestorian Bishop of Al-Basrah early in the XIIIth century.

What exactly were the sources from which the author of the "Cave of Treasures" derived his information it is impossible to say. He was well acquainted with the contents of the Old and New Testaments, and it seems that, either at first hand or through translations, he was familiar with the legends concerning the Creation and the early Patriarchs, which were current among the Hebrews. There is no evidence that he knew Greek, but there is little doubt that much of the information which he gives was derived at second, or third or fourth hand from works written in Greek. Some of these dealt with the history of Babylonia, and the accounts of the early rulers of that country given in them were derived from records written in cuneiform. It is well known that some learned Greeks made their way to Babylon and became acquainted with the history, and religion and language of the country, and then wrote down in their own language the information which they had acquired there at first hand from the native records and chronicles. According to Strabo (XVII. 6) there were several native Babylonians who were acquainted with the Greek language, and he gives the names of some of them, e.g. Kidêna, Naburianos, Sudinos and Seleukos, who were mathematicians and astronomers. And we are justified in assuming that there were also native scholars who dealt with history and chronography, and who either wrote in Greek, as well as cuneiform, or whose works were translated by Greeks who could read the cuneiform inscriptions also.

The section of the "Cave of Treasures" which deals with Abraham, and his father Terah and his grandfather Nâhôr shows that its author's information was based on a more or less historical foundation. The date when Abraham was called by the divine Voice to leave "Ur of the Chaldees " may be placed at about 2000 B.C., i.e. about the time when Khammurabi was making himself master of all Babylonia. In the days of Serug, the great grandfather of Abraham, the worship of idols entered the world. All the people were pagans, and objects celestial and terrestrial were generally worshipped.

The author of the "Cave of Treasures" tells us that at that period men made golden images of their fathers and set them up over their graves, and that the devils who lived in these images called upon the sons of the dead to sacrifice their own sons to them. Now we know from the monuments which have been excavated in Babylonia that in the last centuries of the third millennium B.C. the Babylonians became great experts in the art of sculpture, and that they made images of both men and gods. The excavations have proved that gold masks were laid on the faces of the dead, and we may assume that gold masks were placed on the faces of statues, when they were "dressed" for festival occasions, as in Egypt. Abraham was prepared to sacrifice his son Isaac, according to the custom of his people, but when God stayed his hand, and provided a ram for the blood-sacrifice, he realized that a human blood-sacrifice was not acceptable to Him, and that he must break with the traditions of his people, and leave the country. The custom of sacrificing children to devils seems to have been general in the days of Nâhôr, and it may have been introduced into the country by the hordes who came down from the north as a result of the conquests of Khammurabi. Be this as it may, in the 100th year of the life of Nâhôr God determined to put an end to the custom, and He made the Wind Flood. He opened the storehouses of the winds, and set free the whirlwinds and hurricanes, and sent a blast of wind over all the earth. This wind swept through Babylonia, and dashed the idols against each other, and smashed them, and then it threw down upon them the buildings in which they had stood, and piled up their ruins in high mounds above the images and the devils that dwelt in them. The cities of Ur and Erech were laid waste, and their sites were only known from the huge mounds of rubbish which were piled up by the Wind Flood.

"Amulet formed by the figure of Pazuzu, the
god of storms, cyclones and hurricanes."

Limestone head of the Storm-god
Pazuzu. (British Museum.)

Now there is no record of this Wind Flood in the Bible, and it is only
mentioned in the "Cave of Treasures," and in works based upon it, e.g. the
Book of the Bee and the Book of Adam and Eve. Some light is thrown upon
this Wind Flood by the cuneiform inscriptions, and the author of the "Cave
of Treasures" must have derived his knowledge of it from documents based
upon them. Nabonidus, king of Babylon, displeased the gods, and they
made manifest their anger by making the storm wind to blow. And in one
text it is distinctly said that the cities of Erech and Nippur were destroyed
by a wind storm. (See Sidney Smith, Babylonian Historical Texts, London,
1924, page 93, note 20.) The most terrible of all the storm-wind gods was
Pazuzu, whose strength and violence were believed to be so great that he

could overthrow even the mountains (Revue d'Assyriologie, vol. XI, page 57). Figures of this monster in stone and bronze may be seen in the British Museum.

Terah, the father of Abraham, followed in his father's footsteps, and, according to the legend quoted on page 145, made figures of the gods, or idols, in clay and stone, and sent his son Abraham into the bazâr to sell them. Fact underlies this legend, for a large number of terra-cotta figures of gods and demons have been found by many excavators during the course of their work on the sites of ancient cities in Babylonia; the commonest of these are the so-called "Papsukkal figures," which were believed to protect houses.

"Baked clay figure of the god of the South-east Wind. (British Museum.)"

The materials by which to check the statements made in the "Cave of Treasures" are not available at the present time, but it is very possible that in future years inscribed tablets will be found in Babylonia and Assyria which will contain the original forms of the legends and historical facts that have come down to us. The story of Nimrod and his cult of fire and the white horse, and his visit to the wise man Yôntân, of his skill as a magician, and the cities which he built, may be somewhat garbled, but it is based on genuine historical documents. The narrative of the descents made by Seth and his companions from the mountain of Paradise into the plain is certainly based on historical fact; and though Melchisedek has not yet been identified in the cuneiform inscriptions, there is every reason to believe that he existed, and that he was a founder of a pure form of religion, and a great ruler as well as priest.

The principal object of the writer of the "Cave of Treasures" was to trace the descent of Christ back to Adam, and to show that the Christian Dispensation was foreshadowed in the history of the Patriarchs and their successors the kings of Israel and Judah by means of types and symbols. The Christian Trinity existed before the world and man were made, for "the Spirit of God" which hovered over the waters was the Holy Spirit, and when God said "Let Us make man" by "Us" the Trinity was referred to. The Sabbath was instituted by God Who Himself rested on the seventh day. When Adam stood up upright after his creation he set his feet on the centre of the earth, on the exact spot on which the Cross of our Lord was set up, in Jerusalem. Adam, like Elijah, ascended into heaven in a chariot of fire. The angels carried crosses of light on which the names of the Persons of the Trinity were inscribed, and with them vanquished Satan and his hosts of devils when he rebelled, as the Cross of Christ destroyed the powers of darkness. The Garden of Eden is symbolic of the Holy Church, and as Adam was priest as well as prophet and king, he ministered in it. The Tree of Life prefigured the Cross of Christ, the veritable Tree of Life. On his expulsion from Paradise God told Adam that He would send His Son to redeem him, and ordered him to make arrangements for the embalming of his body and its preservation in the Cave of Treasures.

Adam and Eve lived on bread and wine in Paradise, and Melchisedek administered bread and wine to Abraham, according to the command of Methuselah, and so foreshadowed the institution of the Sacrament. The Cave of Treasures, with the gold, frankincense and myrrh which Adam collected in it, symbolized not only the Temple, or house of prayer, but the cave in which the Magi presented their gifts to Christ. Adam was the first priest, and was present when Cain and Abel made their offerings, and the lamp which he placed by the side of Abel's body in the Cave of Treasures was the prototype of the sanctuary lamp. Adam's body was buried in the Cave of Treasures, which became a family mausoleum, for several of his sons and descendants were also buried there. Noah took Adam's body from the Cave and carried it into Noah's Ark, and it was in due course brought to Jerusalem by him, and deposited in the opening in the earth which the earth itself made to receive it. There it remained until the Cross of Christ was set up above it on Golgotha, and then, when Longinus pierced our Lord's side, the blood and water flowed down into the place where Adam was. The blood gave him life, and he was baptized by the water.

Noah's Ark, bearing the body of Adam, which occupied the centre of it, and divided the men from the women, sailed over the waters until it reached the mountain on which Paradise was situated, and it travelled from east to west, and from north to south, and thus it made the sign of the Cross on the waters of the Flood. When the foremost part of the Flood reached the skirts of the mountain of Paradise, it bowed low and kissed the ground, and then withdrew to continue its work of destruction. The first dove sent out by Noah was a type of the Old Covenant, which was not accepted by the Jews, and the second dove was a type of the New Covenant, which rested on the people through the waters of baptism. One of the legends (see page 147) states that Abraham was circumcised by Gabriel, who was assisted by Michael. Abraham circumcised Isaac, and foresaw the crucifixion of Christ. The angels who were on Jacob's Ladder were Zechariah, and Mary, and the Magi and the Shepherds, and the Lord who stood at the head of it symbolized Christ on the Cross. The watering of the flocks by Jacob at the well symbolized the baptism of the nations. The stone which he set up and anointed was a type of the Christian altar, and the oil he used symbolized the oil used at the Christian altar. The crown of glory which Adam wore prefigured the crown of thorns which was placed on the head of Christ. Adam was three hours in Paradise, and Christ was in Pilate's Hall of Judgment three hours. Adam was naked for three hours, and Christ was naked on the Cross for three hours. The mother of mortal offspring (Eve) proceeded from the right side of Adam, and Baptism, the mother of immortal offspring, went forth from the right side of Christ during His crucifixion.

Adam's descent from Paradise typified the descent of Christ into Sheol; Adam was the prototype of Christ in every respect. Isaac was a symbol of Christ, and the thicket in which the ram, his substitute, was caught symbolized the wood of the Cross. The thread of scarlet of Rahab the harlot typified the red blood of Christ, and the window from which it issued His side. The seamless garment of Christ was the symbol of the indivisible Orthodox Faith.

One of the most important sections of the "Cave of Treasures" is that which contains a description of the Magi and their visit to Jerusalem, for it appears to be based upon the work of some writer who had exact knowledge of their methods. They are here grouped with the Chaldeans, who were presumably Babylonians, but they themselves are called the "wise men of Persia." Both these bodies of sages had studied the motions of the "Malwâshê," or Signs of the Zodiac, for centuries, and through them they felt that they were able to forecast with accuracy the course of events on this earth. The Magi were terrified at the appearance of the star, which led them subsequently to Bethlehem, and thought that the king of the Greeks was about to attack the land of Nimrod. At length they consulted their great astrological work which is here called "Gelyânâ dhe Nemrôdh," i.e. the "Revelation of Nimrod," and there they learned that a king was born in Judah. What this "Revelation of Nimrod" was cannot be said, but it was evidently one of the large series of Omen-texts of which so many examples exist in the British Museum. These texts are being copied and translated by Mr. C. J. Gadd of the British Museum, and when the work is done we may learn something of the book which the Magi consulted. The "Cave of Treasures" says that the Magi were three kings, and gives their names, and thus repeats the tradition which was general in the early centuries of the Christian Era. On the other hand, the "Book of the Bee," following a very ancient Oriental tradition, says they were twelve in number, and gives their names; but it must be noted that some of the names are only found at a comparatively late period of Persian History.

The sources of the genealogy of Christ which is found in the "Cave of Treasures" are unknown, but the author states that he is certain about its correctness, and by inserting it in their copies of the work the scribes have shown that it is worthy of credence. It is probably quite true that when the captain of Nebuchadnezzar's host burnt the books of the Jews after the capture of Jerusalem their tables of genealogy perished with them.

THE FIRST THOUSAND YEARS: ADAM TO YARÊD (Jared)

The Creation. First Day

IN the beginning, on the First Day, which was the holy First Day of the Week, the chief and firstborn of all the days, God created the heavens, and the earth, and the waters, and the air, and the fire, and the hosts which are invisible (that is to say, the Angels, Archangels, Thrones, Lords, Principalities, Powers, Cherubim and Seraphim), and all the ranks and companies of Spiritual beings, and the Light, and the Night, and the Day-time, and the gentle winds and the strong winds (i.e. storms). All these were created on the First Day. And on the First Day of the Week the Spirit of holiness, one of the Persons of the Trinity, hovered over the waters, and through the hovering thereof over the [Fol. 3b, col. 2] face of the waters, the waters were blessed so that they might become producers of offspring, and they became hot, and the whole nature of the waters glowed with heat, and the leaven of creation was united to them. As the mother-bird maketh warm her young by the embrace of her closely covering wings, and the young birds acquire form through the warmth of the heat which [they derive] from her, so through the operation of the Spirit of holiness, the Spirit, the Paraclete, the leaven of the breath of life was united to the waters when He hovered over them.

NOTES.--According to Solomon, a Nestorian bishop of Perâth Mayshân, or Al-Basrah, a city on the right bank of the Shatt al-`Arab, about A.D. 1222, the creation of the heavens and the earth has been planned from everlasting in the immutable mind of God. He created SEVEN substances (or natures) in silence, without voice, viz. heaven, earth, water, air, fire, the angels, and darkness. The earth was plunged in the midst of the waters, above the waters was air, and above the air was fire. Water is cold and moist, air is hot and moist, fire is hot and dry, but it had no luminosity until the Fourth Day, when the luminaries were created. The angels are divided into nine classes and three orders. The upper order contains Cherubim, Seraphim, and Thrones, and these are bearers of God's throne. The middle order contains Lords, Powers, and Rulers. The lower order contains

Principalities, Archangels, and Angels. (Compare the "thrones, or domi-nions, or principalities, or powers" of Col. i. 16.) The Cherubim are an intellectual motion, the Seraphim are a fiery motion, the Thrones are a fixed motion, the Lords are a motion which governs the motions beneath it and controls the devils, the Powers are a motion which gives effect to God's will, the Rulers are a motion which rules spiritual measures and the sun, moon and stars, the Principalities are a motion which rules the elements, the Archangels are a swift operative motion which governs every living creature, except man, and the Angels are a motion which has spiritual knowledge of everything which is in heaven or on the earth. The guardian angel of every man belongs to this last class. The number of each class of angels is equal to the number of all mankind from Adam to the Resurrec-tion. The heaven in which the angels live is above the waters, which are above the firmament, and they minister to their God there, being invisible to bodily eyes. The angels are not self-existent beings--they were created; on the other hand, darkness is a self-existent nature (or substance). Solomon of Al-Basrah does not accept the view that the spirit which hovered over the waters was the Holy Spirit. (See Book of the Bee, ed. Budge, chapters i-vii.)

The Creation. Second Day

And on the Second Day God made the Lower Heaven, and called it REKÎ`A [that is to say, "what is sold and fixed," or "firmament"]. This He did that He might make known that the Lower Heaven doth not possess the nature of the heaven which is above it, and that it is different in appearance from that heaven which is above it, for the heaven above it is of fire. And that second heaven is NÛHRÂ (i.e. Light), and this lower heaven is DARPÎTÎÔN [Fol. 4a, col. 1], and because it hath the dense nature of water it hath been called "Rekî`a." And on the Second Day God made a separation between the waters and the waters, that is to say, between the waters which were above [Rekî`a] and the waters which were below. And the ascent of these waters which were above heaven took place on the Second Day, and they were like unto a dense black cloud of thick darkness. Thus were they raised up there, and they mounted up, and behold, they stand above the Rekî`a in the air; and they do not spread, and they make no motion to any side.

NOTES.--According to the "Book of the Bee," the creation of the firmament enabled God to allot a dwelling place to the angels, where also the souls of the righteous could be received after the General Resurrection. The great abyss of water which God created on the First Day was divided by Him into three parts; one part He left on the earth for the use of man and beast, and to form rivers and seas; of the second part He made the firmament, and the third part the place above the firmament. After the Resurrection all these parts will return to their original state. The word Darpîtîôn is a difficulty, and I cannot explain it. The variant forms Dûrîkôn and Dertêkôn appear in Ethiopic books, wherein it is said to be a name of the sixth heaven.

The Creation. Third Day

And on the Third Day God commanded the waters that were below the firmament (Rekî`a) to be gathered together in one place, and the dry land to appear. And when the covering of water had been rolled up from the face of the earth, the earth showed itself to be in an unsettled and unstable state, that is to say, it was of a damp (or moist) and yielding nature. And the waters were gathered together into seas that were under the earth and within it [Fol. 4a, col. 2], and upon it. And God made in the earth from below, corridors, and shafts, and channels for the passage of the waters; and the winds which come from within the earth ascend by means of these corridors and channels, and also the heat and the cold for the service of the earth. Now, as for the earth, the lower part of it is like unto a thick sponge, for it resteth on the waters. And on this Third Day God commanded the earth, and it brought forth herbs and vegetables, and it conceived in its interior trees, and seeds, and plants and roots.

NOTE.--On this day the waters gathered together in the depths of the earth, sand was set as a limit for the waters of the seas, and the mountains and hills appeared. The sages say that Paradise was created on this day, but the Rabbis held the view that it existed before the world. Solomon of Basrah says that the earth produced herbs and trees by its own power, and that the luminaries had nothing to do with vegetable growth. Book of the Bee (chapter ix.)

The Creation. Fourth Day

And on the Fourth Day God made the sun, and the moon, and the stars. And as soon as the heat of the sun was diffused over the surface of the earth, the earth became hard and rigid, and lost its flaccidity, because the humidity and the dampness [caused by] the waters were taken away from it. The Creator made the sphere of the sun of fire and filled it with light. And God gave unto the sphere of the moon and the stars bodies of water and air, and filled them with light. And when the dust of the earth became hot, it brought forth all the trees [Fol. 4b, col. 1], and plants, and seeds, and roots which had been conceived inside it on the Third Day.

NOTES.--The cases of the sun, moon, and stars were made of aerial material, after the manner of lamps, and God filled them with a mixture of fire, which had no light in it, and with light which had no heat in it. The path of the luminaries is beneath the firmament; they are not fixed, as the ignorant think, but are guided in their courses by the angels. The Ethiopians have a tradition that when the sun was first made its light was twelve times as strong as it is to-day. The angels complained that the heat was too strong, and that it hampered them in the performance of their duties, whereupon God divided it into twelve parts, and took away six of these parts, and out of three of them He made the moon and stars, and the other three He distributed among the waters, the clouds, and the lightning.

The Creation. Fifth Day

And on the Fifth Day God commanded the waters, and they brought forth all kind of fish of divers appearances, and creatures which move about, and twist themselves and wriggle in the waters, and serpents, and Leviathan, and beasts of terrible aspects, and feathered fowl of the air and of the waters. And on this same day God made from the earth all the cattle and wild beasts, and all the reptiles which creep about upon the earth.

NOTES.--According to the Book of the Bee (chapter xii), beasts and animals were created on Friday evening, and they can therefore see at night as well as in the daytime. In the Book of Mysteries of Heaven and Earth, "whales" and the Behemôth are mentioned with Leviathan.

The Creation. Sixth Day

And on the Sixth Day, which is the Eve of the Sabbath, God formed man out of the dust, and Eve from his rib.

And on the Seventh Day God rested from His labours, and it is called "Sabbath."

The Creation of Adam

Now the formation of Adam took place in this wise: On the Sixth Day, which is the Eve of the Sabbath, at the first hour of the day, when quietness was reigning over [Fol. 4b, col. 2] all the Ranks [of the Angels], and the hosts [of heaven], God said, "Come ye, let Us make man in Our image, and according to Our likeness." Now by this word "Us" He maketh known concerning the Glorious Persons [of the Trinity]. And when the angels heard this utterance, they fell into a state of fear and trembling, and they said to one another, "A mighty miracle will be made manifest to us this day [that is to say], the likeness of God, our Maker." And they saw the right hand of God opened out flat, and stretched out over the whole world; and all creatures were collected in the palm of His right hand. And they saw that He took from the whole mass of the earth one grain of dust, and from the whole nature of water one drop of water, and from all the air which is above one puff of wind, and from the whole nature of fire a little of its heat and warmth. And the angels saw that when these four feeble (or inert) materials were placed in the palm of His right hand [Fol. 5a, col. 1], that is to say, cold, and heat, and dryness, and moisture, God formed Adam. Now, for what reason did God make Adam out of these four materials unless it were [to show] that everything which is in the world should be in subordination to him through them? He took a grain from the earth in order that everything in nature which is formed of earth should be subject unto him; and a drop of water in order that everything which is in the seas and rivers should be his; and a puff of air so that all kinds [of creatures] which fly in the air might be given unto him; and the heat of fire so that all the beings that are fiery in nature, and the celestial hosts, might be his helpers.

God formed Adam with His holy hands, in His own Image and Likeness, and when the angels saw Adam's glorious appearance they were greatly moved by the beauty thereof. For they saw [Fol. 5a, col. 2] the image of his face burning with glorious splendour like the orb of the sun, and the light of his eyes was like the light of the sun, and the image of his body was like unto the sparkling of crystal. And when he rose at full length and stood upright in the centre of the earth, he planted his two feet on that spot whereon was set up the Cross of our Redeemer; for Adam was created in Jerusalem. There he was arrayed in the apparel of sovereignty, and there was the crown of glory set upon his head, there was he made king, and priest, and prophet, there did God make him to sit upon his honourable throne, and there did God give him dominion over all creatures and things. And all the wild beasts, and all the cattle, and the feathered fowl were gathered together, and they passed before Adam and he assigned names to them; and they bowed their heads before him; and eveything in nature worshipped him [Fol. 5b, col. 1], and submitted themselves unto him. And the angels and the hosts of heaven heard the Voice of God saying unto him, "Adam, behold; I have made thee king, and priest, and prophet, and lord, and head, and governor of everything which hath been made and created; and they shall be in subjection unto thee, and they shall be thine, and I have given unto thee power over everything which I have created." And when the angels heard this speech they all bowed the knee and worshipped Him.

NOTES.--The Jews consider that the words, "Come, let Us make man," refer to God and the angels, but the Fathers of the Syrian Church understand that God refers to the Three Persons of the Trinity. Some Fathers believe that Adam was formed on the morning of the Sixth Day, outside Paradise, but others think that the formation of Adam took place in the evening in Paradise. According to some, Paradise was created before the world, and, according to others, on the Third Day. Bar Hebraeus says that Adam was created on Friday of the first week of Nîsân (April), the first month of the first year of the world. The Egyptian and Ethiopian Churches have a tradition that the angels were not all created at the same time. The great archangel Michael, who is called the "Angel of the Face," and all his Rank of angels were created in the first hour of Friday, the Priests in the second, the Thrones in the third, the Dominions (or Sultâns) in the fourth, the Lords in the fifth, the Powers in the sixth, the Tens of Thousands in the seventh, the Governors in the eighth, the Masters in the ninth. After the Governors the Rank of angels governed by Satan were created, and then the Tenth Rank.

According to a Coptic tradition preserved in the Discourse on Abbatôn, the Angel of Death, by Timothy, Archbishop of Rakoti (Alexandria), the clay of which Adam was made was brought by the angel Mûrîêl from the Land of the East. When God had made his body He left it lying for forty days and forty nights without putting breath into it. At the request of our Lord, Who promised to become Adam's advocate and to go down into the world, God breathed into Adam's nostrils the breath of life three times, saying, "Live! Live! Live! according to the type of My Divinity." Thereupon Adam rose up, and worshipped the Father, saying, "My Lord and my God." (Budge, Coptic Martyrdoms, page 482.)

THE REVOLT OF SATAN, AND THE BATTLE IN HEAVEN

And when the prince of the lower order of angels saw what great majesty had been given unto Adam, he was jealous of him from that day, and he did not wish to worship him. And he said unto his hosts, "Ye shall not worship him, and ye shall not praise him with the angels. It is meet that ye should worship me, because I am fire and spirit; and not that I should worship a thing of dust, which hath been fashioned of fine dust." And the Rebel meditating these things [Fol. 5b, col. 2] would not render obedience to God, and of his own free will he asserted his independence and separated himself from God. But he was swept away out of heaven and fell, and the fall of himself and of all his company from heaven took place on the Sixth Day, at the second hour of the day. And the apparel of their glorious state was stripped off them. And his name was called "Sâtânâ" because he turned aside [from the right way], and "Shêdâ" because he was cast out, and "Daiwâ" because he lost the apparel of his glory. And behold, from that time until the present day, he and all his hosts have been stripped of their apparel, and they go naked and have horrible faces. And when Sâtânâ was cast out from heaven, Adam was raised up so that he might ascend to Paradise in a chariot of fire. And the angels went before him, singing praises, and the Seraphim ascribed holiness unto him, and the Cherubim ascribed blessing; and amid cries of joy and praises Adam went into [Fol. 6a, col. 1] Paradise. And as soon as Adam entered Paradise he was commanded not to eat of a [certain] tree; his entrance into heaven took place at the third hour of the Eve of the Sabbath (i.e. on Friday morning).

NOTES.--The Fathers of the Egyptian and Ethiopian Churches treat the story of the Fall of Satan in great detail. According to them, Satan, or Satnâêl, was greatly astonished at the beauty and splendour of the sun and moon, and on the Fourth Day of the week he declared to himself that he would set his throne above the stars, and make himself equal to God. One week after the creation of Adam, Satan declared war on the hosts of Almighty God. These were commanded by Michael and consisted of 120,000 horsemen, 600,000 shield bearers, 700,000 mail-clad horsemen in chariots of fire, 700,000 torch bearers, 800,000 angels with daggers of fire, 1,000,000 slingers, 500,000 bearers of axes of fire, 300,000 bearers of fiery crosses, and 400,000 bearers of lamps. The angels uttered their battle cries and began to fight, but Satan charged them and dispersed them; they reformed, but again Satan charged them and put them to flight. Then God gave the angels the Cross of Light, which bore the legend, "In the Name of the Father, and the Son, and the Holy Ghost." And when they attacked the hosts of darkness under this Cross, Satan became faint, and he and his forces withdrew, and Michael hurled them down into hell. The Abyssinian legend says that Satan was 1,700 cubits high, and his hand 70 cubits long, and his foot 7,000 cubits long; his mouth was 40 cubits in width, his face was as broad as the distance of a day's journey, and the length of his eyebrows was a distance of three days' journey. [From the Book of the Mysteries of Heaven and Earth.] The prototype of the great fight in heaven between the powers of light and darkness is found in ancient Egyptian religious texts, in more than one form. In the oldest form Set, , the Devil, rebels against Her-ur, , the god of heaven, whose chief symbols are the sun and moon, and is utterly defeated. In the next form Set $\Box$ attacks the Sun-god R⁻a, , and $\Box$ is destroyed by him; the great ally of Set, called ⁻Apep (Apôphis), , and $\Box$ $\Box$ all his fiends and devils (the Sebau), $\Box$, are defeated and burnt up daily. In another form Set makes war on Horus, the son of Osiris, and on Osiris himself, and is defeated utterly. The Coptic version of the legend was borrowed from the old hieroglyphic texts, and then Christianized. Compare the following:--

When Satan saw Adam seated on a great throne, with a crown of glory on his head and a sceptre in his hand, and all the angels worshipping him, he was filled with anger. And when God said to him, "Come thou also, for thou shalt worship My image and likeness," Satan refused to do so, and, assuming an arrogant and insolent manner, he said, "It is meet that he should worship me, for I existed before he came into being." When the Father saw his overbearing attitude, He knew that Satan's wickedness and rebellion had reached their highest pitch. He ordered the celestial soldiers to take from him the written authority that was in his hand, to strip off his armour, and to hurl him down from heaven to earth. Satan was the greatest of the angels, and God had made him the Commander-in-Chief of the celestial hosts, and in the document which Satan held in his hand were written the names of all the angels under his command. Knowing their names, his authority over them was absolute. When God saw that the angels hesitated to take the document from him, He commanded them to bring a sharp reaping-knife, and to stab him on this side and that, right through his body to the backbone and shoulder blades; and Satan could no longer stand upright. And a Cherub smote him, and broke his wings and his ribs, and having rendered him helpless he cast Satan down from Heaven upon the earth. Then he became the Arch-Devil and the leader of those who were cast out of heaven with him, and who henceforth were devils. (From Budge, Coptic Martyrdoms, page 484.)]

THE MAKING OF EVE

And God cast a sleep upon Adam and he slept. And God took a rib from the loins on the right side of Adam, and He made Khâwâ (i.e. Eve) from it; and when Adam woke up, and saw Eve, he rejoiced in her greatly. And Adam and Eve were in Paradise, and clothed with glory and shining with praise for three hours. Now this Paradise was situated on a high range of hills, and it was thirty spans--according to the measurement of the spirit--higher than all the high mountains, and it surrounded the whole earth.

NOTES.--God did not make Eve of earth, that she might not be considered something alien to Adam in nature; and He did not take her from Adam's fore-parts, that she might not uplift herself against him; nor from his hind-parts, that she might not be accounted despicable; nor from his right side, that she might not have pre-eminence over him; nor from his head, that she might not seek authority over him; nor from his feet, that she might not be trodden down and scorned in the eyes of her husband; but [He took her] from his left side, for the side is the place which unites and joins both front and back (Book of the Bee, chapter xiv, and Bar Hebraeus, Ausar Râzê). Further, God did not form Eve from Adam's head, that she might not carry her head proudly; nor from his eye, that she might not be curious; nor from his ear, that she might not be an eavesdropper; nor from his mouth, that she might not be gossiping; nor from his heart, that she might not be quarrelsome; nor from his hand, that she might not touch everything with her hand; nor from his feet, that she might not rove about (Berêshîth Rabbah on Gen. ii. 23).

Now Moses the prophet said that God planted Paradise in Eden and placed Adam there (Gen. ii. 8).

NOTES.--Paradise was situated on Mount Eden, beyond the Ocean, and it was filled with fruit-bearing trees. The great river which sprung up in it was parted into four heads, viz. PISHÔN, which flowed through Havilâ, where there were beryls, and gold, and stones of price; GÎHÔN, or the Nile of Egypt; DEKLATH (the Tigris), which flows through Assyria; and PERATH (the

Euphrates). The keepers of Paradise were Enoch and Elijah, and in it dwelt the souls of the righteous. The souls of sinners dwelt in a deep place, outside Eden. The tree of good and evil that was in Paradise did not possess these properties naturally, but only through the deed which was wrought by its means. Adam and Eve did not become naked and die the death of sin because they desired and ate of the fruit of the fig-tree, but because they transgressed the law. The tree of which they ate may have been the fig-tree, or the date-palm, or the vine or the ethrôg (citron). Mount Eden is probably the original of Jabal Kâf of the Arabs, a mountain range which surrounds the whole world.

THE SYMBOLISM OF EDEN

Now Eden is the Holy Church, and the Church [Fol. 6a, col. 2] is the compassion of God, which He was about to extend to the children of men. For God, according to His foreknowledge, knew what Satan had devised against Adam, and therefore He set Adam beforehand in the bosom of His compassion, even as the blessed David singeth concerning Him in the Psalm (xc), saying, "Lord, Thou hast been an abiding place for us throughout all generations," that is to say, "Thou hast made us to have our abiding place in Thy compassion." And, when entreating God on behalf of the redemption of the children of men, David said, "Remember Thy Church, which Thou didst acquire in olden time " (Ps. lxxiv. 2), that is to say, "[Remember] Thy compassion, which Thou art about to spread over our feeble race." Eden is the Holy Church, and the Paradise which was in it is the land of rest, and the inheritance of life, which God hath prepared for all the holy children of men. And because [Fol. 6b, col. 1] Adam was priest, and king, and prophet, God brought him into Paradise that he might minister in Eden, the Holy Church, even as the blessed man Moses testifieth concerning him, saying, "That he might serve God by means of priestly ministration with praise, and that he might keep that commandment which had been entrusted to him by the compassion of God" (Gen. ii. 15, 16 ?). And God made Adam and Eve to dwell in Paradise. True is this word, and it proclaimeth the truth: That Tree of Life which was in the midst of Paradise prefigured the Redeeming Cross, which is the veritable Tree of Life, and this it was that was fixed in the middle of the earth.

SATAN'S ATTACK ON ADAM AND EVE

And when Satan saw that Adam and Eve were happy and joyful in Paradise, that Rebel was smitten sorely with jealousy, and he became filled with wrath. And he went and took up his abode in the serpent, and he raised him up, and made him to fly through the air to the skirts of Mount [Eden] whereon was Paradise [Fol. 6b, col. 2]. Now, why did Satan enter the body of the serpent and hide himself therein? Because he knew that his appearance was foul, and that if Eve saw his form, she would betake herself to flight straightway before him. Now, the man who wished to teach the Greek language to a bird--now the bird that can learn the speech of men is called "babbaghah" (i.e. parrot)--first bringeth a large mirror and placeth between himself and the bird. He then beginneth to talk to the bird, and immediately the parrot heareth the voice of the man, it turneth round, and when it seeth its own form [reflected] in the mirror, it becometh pleased straightway, because it imagineth that a fellow parrot is talking to it. Then it inclineth its ear with pleasure, and listeneth to the words of the man who is talking to it, and it becometh eager to learn, and to speak Greek. In this manner (i.e. with the object of making Eve believe that it was the serpent that spoke to her) did Satan enter in and dwell in the serpent, and he watched for the opportunity, and [when] he saw Eve by herself [Fol. 7a, col. 1], he called her by her name. And when she turned round towards him, she saw her own form [reflected] in him, and she talked to him; and Satan led her astray with his lying words, because the nature of woman is soft (or, yielding).

And when Eve had heard from him concerning that tree, straightway she ran quickly to it, and she plucked the fruit of disobedience from the tree of transgression of the command, and she ate. Then immediately she found herself stripped naked, and she saw the hatefulness of her shame, and she ran away naked, and hid herself in another tree, and covered her naked-ness with the leaves thereof. And she cried out to Adam, and he came to her, and she handed to him some of the fruit of which she had eaten, and he also did eat thereof. And when he had eaten he also became naked, and he and Eve made girdles for their loins of the leaves of the fig-trees; and they were arrayed in these girdles of ignominy for three [Fol. 7a, col. 2] hours. At mid-day they received [their] sentence of doom. And God made for them tunics of skin which was stripped from the trees, that is to say, of the bark of the trees, because the trees that were in Paradise had soft barks, and they were softer than the byssus and silk wherefrom the garments worn by kings are made. And God dressed them in this soft skin, which was thus spread over a body of infirmities.

NOTES.--The Fathers of the Ethiopian Church emphasize the difficulty which Satan found in entering Paradise. He knew that he could not carry out his plan for ruining Adam if he entered Paradise in his own form, and he decided that he must assume the form of some bird or animal or reptile if he was to succeed. He applied to the white bird Arzel, and the green bird Besel, and a red bird, but each refused to take him to the place where Eve was. Then he applied to the elephant, and the lion, and the leopard, and the hyena, and the wild boar; the first four refused point blank to do what Satan wished, and the wild boar attempted to gore him with his tusks. On this Satan took to flight. He then went to the animal Sereg, which was commonly known as the "digger of graves," but this animal refused to help him, and then Satan approached the animal called "Taman," "the front part of which was like a camel's foal." This creature agreed to help him, and, mounted on his back, Satan entered Paradise and stood before Eve. The serpent became spokesman for him, and Eve hearkened to him and ate of the fruit. According to the "Book of the Mysteries of Heaven and Earth," the tree was called "Sezen," and each fruit cluster contained, 150,000 grains, or berries. It is described as a large and handsome tree, and it has been identified with the "Sendâlê," or sandal-wood tree. According to the same authorities, the Tree of Life was the prototype of the Cross on which our Lord was crucified.

Adam's stay in Paradise

At the third hour of the day Adam and Eve ascended into Paradise, and for three hours they enjoyed the good things thereof; for three hours they were in shame and disgrace, and at the ninth hour their expulsion from Paradise took place. And as they were going forth sorrowfully, God spake unto Adam, and heartened him, and said unto him, "Be not sorrowful, O Adam, for I will restore unto thee thine inheritance. Behold, see how greatly I have loved thee, for though I have cursed the earth for thy sake, yet have I withdrawn thee from the operation of the curse. As for the serpent [Fol. 7b, col. 1], I have fettered his legs in his belly, and I have given him the dust of the earth for food; and Eve have I bound under the yoke of servitude. Inasmuch as thou hast transgressed my commandments get thee forth, but be not sad. After the fulfilment of the times which I have allotted that you shall be in exile outside [Paradise], in the land which is under the curse, behold, I will send my Son. And He shall go down [from heaven] for thy redemption, and He shall sojourn in a Virgin, and shall put on a body [of flesh], and through Him redemption and a return shall be effected for thee. But command thy sons, and order them to embalm thy body after thy death with myrrh, cassia, and stakte. And they shall place thee in this cave, wherein I am making you to dwell this day, until the time when your expulsion shall take place from the regions of Paradise to that earth which is outside it. And whosoever shall be left in those days shall take thy body with him, and [Fol. 7b, col. 2] shall deposit it on the spot which I shall show him, in the centre of the earth; for in that place shall redemption be effected for thee and for all thy children." And God revealed unto Adam everything which the Son would suffer on behalf of him.

Adam's expulsion from Paradise

And when Adam and Eve had gone forth from Paradise, the door of Paradise was shut, and a cherub bearing a two-edged sword stood by it. According to the Book of the Bee, the cherub, or, as some think, a "terrible form endowed with a body," was armed with a spear and sword, each being made of fire.

And Adam and Eve went down in . . . . of spirit over the mountains of Paradise, and they found a cave in the top of the mountain, and they entered and hid themselves therein.

NOTES.--When Adam and Eve left Paradise they no longer had fruit and wine and bread and flesh to live upon, and they subsisted on cooked grain and vegetables and the herbs of the earth, of which they ate sparingly. Moreover, the four-footed beasts and fowl and reptiles rebelled against them, and some of them became enemies and adversaries unto them. Book of the Bee (chapter xvii.)

Now Adam and Eve were virgins, and Adam wished to know Eve his wife. And Adam took from the skirts of the mountain of Paradise, gold, and myrrh, and frankincense, and he placed them in the cave, and he blessed the cave, and consecrated it that it might be the house of prayer for himself and his sons. And he called the cave "ME`ÂRATH GAZZÊ" (i.e. "CAVE OF TREASURES") [Fol. 8a, col. 1].

So Adam and Eve went down from that holy mountain [of Eden] to the slopes which were below it, and there Adam knew Eve his wife. [A marginal note in the manuscript says that Adam knew Eve thirty years after they went forth from Paradise.] And Eve conceived and brought forth Cain and Lebhûdhâ, his sister, with him; and Eve conceived again and she brought forth Hâbhîl (Abel) and Kelîmath, his sister, with him. [The Book of the Bee makes Kelîmath the twin sister of Cain, and Lebhûdhâ the twin sister of Abel.] And when the children grew up, Adam said unto Eve, "Let Cain take to wife Kelîmath, who was brought forth with Abel, and let Abel take to wife Lebhûdhâ, who was brought forth with Cain." And Cain said unto Eve his mother, "I will take to wife my twin sister Lebhûdhâ, and let Abel take to wife his twin sister Kelîmath"; now Lebhûdhâ was beautiful. When Adam heard these words, which were exceedingly displeasing unto him, he said, "It will be a transgression of the commandment for thee to take [to wife] thy sister, who was born with thee. Nevertheless, take ye to yourselves fruits of trees, and the young of sheep, and get ye up to the top [Fol. 8a, col. 2] of this holy mountain. Then go ye into the Cave of Treasures, and offer ye up your offerings, and make your prayers, and then ye shall consort with your wives." And it came to pass that when Adam, the first priest, and Cain and Abel, his sons, were going up to the top of the mountain, Satan entered into Cain [and persuaded him] to kill Abel, his brother, because of Lebhûdhâ; and because his offering was rejected and was not accepted before God, whilst the offering of Abel was accepted, Cain's jealousy of his brother Abel was increased. And when they came down to the plain, Cain rose up against his brother Abel, and he killed him with a blow from a stone of flint. Then straightway Cain received the doom of death, instead of curses, and he became a fugitive and a wanderer all the days of his life. And God drove him forth into exile in a certain part of the forest of Nôdh, and Cain took to wife his twin sister and made the place of his abode there.

NOTES.--Adam carried Abel to the Cave of Treasures and buried him therein, and he set by the side of the body a lamp which burned day and night. Abel was fifteen and a half years old when Cain, who was seventeen and a half years old, murdered him. Adam and Eve mourned for Abel, in great grief, for one hundred and forty days. Book of Adam and Eve (II, 1.)

The Birth of Seth

And Adam and Eve mourned for Abel [Fol. 8b, col. 1] one hundred years (sic). And then Adam knew his wife again, and she brought forth Seth, the Beautiful, a man mighty and perfect like unto Adam, and he became the father of the mighty men who lived before the Flood.

NOTES.--Seth was born in the 130th year of Adam's life (Gen. v. 3), but the Book of the Bee says it was the 230th year. Adam and Seth and his sons dwelt on the top of Mount Eden, while Cain and his children lived on the plain below.

The Posterity of Seth

And to Seth was born Ânôsh (Enos), and Ânôsh begot Kainân (Cainan), and Kainân begot Mahlâlâîl (Mahalaleel); these [are] the Patriarchs who were born in the days of Adam.

The Death of Adam

And when Adam had lived nine hundred and thirty years, that is to say, until the one hundred and thirty-fifth year of Mahlâlâîl, the day of his death drew nigh and came. And Seth, his son, and Ânôsh, and Kainân, and Mahlâlâîl gathered themselves together and came to him. And they were blessed by him, and he prayed over them. And he commanded his son Seth, and said unto him, "Observe, my son Seth, that which I command thee this day, and do thou on the day of thy death give my command to Ânôsh, and repeat it to him, and let him repeat it to Kainân, and Kainân shall repeat it to Mahlâlâîl [Fol. 8b, col. 2], and let this [my] command be handed on to all your generations. And when I die, embalm me with myrrh, and cassia, and stakte, and deposit my body in the Cave of Treasures. And whosoever shall be left of your generations in that day, when your going forth from this country, which is round about Paradise, shall take place, shall carry my body with him, and shall take it and deposit it in the centre of the earth, for in that place shall redemption be effected for me and for all my children. And be thou, O my son Seth, governor of the sons of thy people. And thou shalt rule them purely and holily in an the fear of God. And keep ye your offspring separate from the offspring of Cain, the murderer."

And when the report "Adam is dying" was known generally, all his offspring gathered together, and came to him, that is to say, Seth, his son, and Ânôsh, and Kainân and Mahlâlâîl, they and their wives [Fol. 9a, col. 1], and their sons, and their daughters; and Adam blessed them. And the departure of Adam from this world took place in the nine hundred and thirtieth year--according to the reckoning from the beginning--on the fourteenth day of the moon, on the sixth day of the month of Nîsân (April), at the ninth hour, on the day of the Eve of the Sabbath (i.e. Friday). At the same hour in which the Son of Man delivered up his soul to His Father on the Cross, did our father Adam deliver up his soul to Him that fashioned him; and he departed from this world.

The Burial of Adam

And when Adam was dead his son Seth embalmed him, according as Adam had commanded him, with myrrh, and cassia, and stakte; now Adam's dead body was the first [body buried] in the earth. And grief for him was exceedingly sore, and Seth [and his sons] mourned for his death one hundred and forty days; and they took Adam's body up to the top of the mountain, and buried it in the Cave of Treasures. And after the families and peoples of the childreh of Seth had buried Adam, they separated themselves from the children of Cain, the murderer. And Seth took Ânôsh [Fol. 9a, col. 2], his firstborn, and Kainân, and Mahlâlâîl, and their wives and children, and led them up into the glorious mountain where Adam was buried; and Cain and all his descendants remained below on the plain where Cain slew Abel.

The Rule of Seth

And Seth became the governor of the children of his people, and he ruled them in purity and holiness. And because of their purity they received the name, which is the best of all names, and were called "the sons of God," they and their wives and their sons. Thus they lived in that mountain in all purity and holiness and in the fear of God. And they went up on the skirts of [the mountain] of Paradise, and they became praisers and glorifiers of God in the place of that host of devils who fell from heaven. There they dwelt in peace and happiness: there was nothing about which they needed to feel anxiety, they had nothing to weary or trouble them [Fol. 9b, col. 1], and they had nothing to do except to praise and glorify God, with the angels. For they heard continually the voices of the angels who were singing praises in Paradise, which was situated at no great height above them--in fact, only about thirty spans—according to the measure of the spirit. They suffered neither toil nor fatigue, they had neither seed [time] nor harvest, but they fed themselves with the delectable fruits of glorious trees of all kinds, and they enjoyed the sweet scent and perfume of the breezes which were wafted forth to them from Paradise. [Thus lived] those holy men, who were indeed holy, and their wives were pure, and their sons were virtuous, and their daughters were chaste and undefiled. In them there was no rebellious thought, no envy, no anger, no enmity. In their wives and daughters there was no impure longing, and neither lasciviousness [Fol. 9b, col. 2], nor cursing, nor lying was heard among them. The only oath which they used in swearing was, "By the blood of Abel." And they, and their wives, and their children used to rise up early in the morning, and go up to the top of that holy mountain, and worship there before God. And they were blessed by the body of Adam their father, and they lifted up their eyes to Paradise, and praised God; and thus they did all the days of their life.

NOTES.--According to the Book of the Bee (chapter xviii), Adam lived 930 years, and Seth lived 913 or 905 years. Seth was 250 years old (105 years in Gen. v. 6) when he begot Enos. "In the days of Seth the knowledge of books went forth in the earth; but the Church does not accept this." According to the Book of Adam (ii. 5), Seth knew good and evil when he was seven years of age, and he spent his days and nights in fasting and prayer, and he made an offering to God daily. Satan appeared to him, and tried to persuade him to leave the holy mountain, and to go and live with him, and to marry one of his women, but Seth resisted him; and mounting the altar of God, drove him away. When Seth was fifteen years old Adam married him to Aklia, the sister of Abel, and when he was twenty years old he begot Enos.

And when Seth had lived nine hundred and thirteen years he became sick unto death. And Ânôsh his son, and Kainân, and Mahlâlâîl, and Yârêd (Jared), and Henôkh (Enoch), and their wives and their sons, gathered together and came unto him, and they were blessed by him. And he prayed over them, and commanded them, and made them to take an oath, and said unto them [Fol. 10a, col. 1], "I will make you to take an oath, and to swear by the holy blood of Abel, that none of you will go down from this holy mountain to the children of Cain, the murderer. For ye know well the enmity which hath existed between us and Cain from the day whereon he slew Abel." And Seth blessed Ânôsh, his son; and gave him commands concerning the body of Adam, and he made him ruler over the children of his people. And Seth ruled them in purity and in holiness, and he ministered diligently before the body of Adam. And Seth died when he was nine hundred and twelve years old, on the seven-and-twentieth day of the blessed month of Âbh (August), on the second day of the week (Monday), at the third hour, in the twentieth year of the life of Enoch. And Ânôsh,

Seth's first-born son, embalmed his body and buried him in the Cave of Treasures, with his father Adam; and they made a mourning for him forty [Fol. 10a, col. 2] days.

NOTES.--The Book of Adam (ii. 12) says that Seth was embalmed with sweet spices, and laid on the right side of Adam's body, but there is no evidence that the Hebrews were acquainted with the art of mummification before they had intercourse with Egypt.

The Rule of Ânôsh

And Ânôsh rose up to minister before God in the Cave of Treasures. And he became the governor of the children of his people, and he kept all the commandments which his father Seth had commanded him, and he urged them to be constant in prayer.

NOTES.--According to the Book of the Bee (chapter xviii), Ânôsh was two hundred and ninety (ninety years in Gen. v. 9) years old when he begot Kainân; and Ânôsh first called upon the name of the Lord. Some say that he first composed books upon the course of the stars and the signs of the Zodiac.

And in the days of Ânôsh, in his eight hundred and twentieth year, Lamech, the blind man, killed Cain, the murderer, in the Forest of Nôdh. Now this killing took place in the following manner. As Lamech was leaning on the youth, his son [Tubal-Cain], and the youth was setting straight his father's arm in the direction in which he saw the quarry, he heard the sound of Cain moving about, backwards and forwards, in the forest. Now Cain was unable to stand still in one place and to hold his peace. And Lamech, thinking that it was a wild beast that was making a movement in the forest, raised his arm, and, having made ready, drew his bow and shot an arrow [Fol. 10b, col. 1] towards that spot, and the arrow smote Cain between his eyes, and he fell down and died. And Lamech, thinking that he had shot game, spake to the youth, saying, "Make haste, and let us see what game we have shot." And when they went to the spot, and the boy on whom Lamech leaned had looked, he said unto him, "O my lord, thou hast killed Cain." And Lamech moved his hands to smite them together, and as he did so he smote the youth and killed him also.

NOTES.--The Book of Adam (ii. 13) says that Lamech was armed with a bow and large arrows, and a sling and smooth stones. An arrow pierced one side of Cain, and a stone from Lamech's sling knocked out both his eyes. Lamech smote the youth who led him about accidentally, but afterwards he smashed his head in with a stone. There are many versions of the story in Arabic, Ethiopic, and Hebrew, but they all agree in essential details. According to the Book of the Bee (chapter xviii), the anvil and hammer and tongs were invented by Tubal-Cain and Jubal, who also constructed musical instruments, harps and pipes; devils lived in the pipes, and sang therein.

And when Ânôsh had lived nine hundred and five years, and was sick unto death, all the patriarchs gathered themselves together, and came unto him, viz. Kainân, his first-born son, and Mahlâlâîl, and Yârêd, and Enoch, and Matûshlah (Methuselah), they, and their wives, and their sons. And they were blessed by him, and he prayed over them and commanded them, and spake unto them, saying, "I will make you to swear by the holy blood of Abel that not one of you shall go down from this mountain to the plain, nor into the encampment of [Fol. 10b, col. 2] the children of Cain, the murderer; and ye shall not mingle yourselves among them. Take ye good heed unto this matter, for ye well know what enmity hath existed between us and them from the day whereon Cain slew Abel." And he blessed Kainân, his son, and commanded him concerning the body of Adam, that he should minister before it all the days of his life, and that he should rule over the children of his people in purity and holiness. And Ânôsh died at the age of nine hundred and five years, on the third day of the month of the First Teshrîn (October), on the day of the Sabbath, in the fifty-third year of the life of Methuselah. And Kainân, his first-born, embalmed him and buried him in the Cave of Treasures, with Adam and Seth, his father. And they made a mourning for him forty days.

NOTES.--The Book of Adam (ii. 14) says that Ânôsh was 985 years old when he died, and that he was laid on the left-hand side of Adam in the Cave of Treasures.

The Rule of Kainân

And Kainân stood up before God to minister in the Cave of Treasures. He was an honourable and pure man, and he governed the children of his people in the complete [Fol. 11a, col. 1] fear of God, and he fulfilled all the commandments of Ânôsh his father. And when Kainân had lived nine hundred and twenty years [in the Book of Adam and the Book of the Bee 910 years], and was sick unto death, all the Patriarchs gathered together and came unto him, viz. Mahlâlâîl his son, and Yârêd, and Enoch and Methuselah and Lamech, they and their wives and their children, and were blessed by him. And he prayed over them and commanded them, saying, "I will make you swear by the holy blood of Abel that not one of you shall go down from this holy mountain into the camp of the children of Cain, the murderer, for ye all know well what enmity hath existed between us and them since the day whereon he killed Abel." And he blessed his son Mahlâlâîl, and admonished him concerning the body of Adam, and said unto him, "Behold, O my son Mahlâlâîl, minister thou before God in purity and holiness [Fol. 11a, col. 2] in the Cave of Treasures, and depart not thou from the presence of the body of Adam all the days of thy life. And be thou the governor of the children of thy people, and rule thou them purely and holily." Kainân died, being nine hundred and twenty years old, on the thirteenth day of the month of Hezêrân (June), on the fourth day of the week (Wednesday), at mid-day, in the five and sixtieth year of [the life of] Lamech, the father of Noah. And Mahlâlâîl, his son, embalmed him, and buried him in the Cave of Treasures; and they made mourning for him forty days.

NOTES.--According to Gen. v. 12, Kainân was 70 years old when he begot Mahlâlâîl, but the Book of the Bee gives 140 years. The Book of Adam says that the people made "offerings for him, after the custom of their fathers," a statement that seems to suggest that the Hebrews not only mummified their dead, but presented funerary offerings to them, after the manner of the Egyptians.

The Rule of Mahlâlâîl

And Mahlâlâîl rose up and ministered before God in the place of Kainân his father. He was constant in prayer by day and by night, and he urged earnestly the children of his people to observe holiness and purity, and to pray without ceasing. And when Mahlâlâîl had lived eight hundred and ninety-five years [Fol. 11b, col. 1], and the day of his departure drew nigh, and he was sick unto death, all the Patriarchs gathered together and came unto him, viz. Yârêd, his first-born, and Enoch and Methuselah, and Lamech, and Noah, they and their wives and their children, and were blessed by him. And he prayed over them, and commanded them, saying, "I will make you to swear by the holy blood of Abel, that not one of you shall go down from this holy mountain. And ye shall not permit any one of your descendants to go down to the plain, to the children of Cain, the murderer, for ye all well know what enmity hath existed between us and them from the day whereon he slew Abel." And he blessed Yârêd, his first-born, and he commanded him concerning the body of Adam, and revealed unto him the place whereto he should make ready to go. And he also commanded him, and made him to swear an oath, saying, "Thou shalt not depart from the body of our father Adam all the days of thy life, and thou shalt be [Fol. 11b, col. 2] the governor of the children of thy people, and shalt rule them in chastity and holiness." And Mahlâlâîl died, [being] eight hundred and ninety-five years old, on the second day of the month Nîsân (April), on the first day of the week (Sunday), at the third hour of the day, in the four and thirtieth year of the life of Noah. And Yârêd, his first-born, embalmed him, and buried him in the Cave of Treasures; and the people made a mourning for him forty days.

NOTES.--According to Gen. v. 15, Mahlâlâîl was 65 years old when he begot Yârêd, but the Book of the Bee gives 165 years; the Book of Adam (ii. 16) says he fell sick when he was 870 years old. The latter work makes the Patriarch tell Yârêd that the people will go down from the mountain, and mingle with the children of Cain, and perish with them.

The Rule of Yârêd

And Yârêd his son rose up and ministered before God [in the Cave of Treasures]. He was a perfect man, and was complete in all the virtues, and he was constant in prayer by day and by night. And because of the excellence of his life and conversation, his days were longer than those of all the children of his people. And in the days of Yârêd, in the five hundredth year of his life, the children of Seth broke the oaths which their fathers had made them to swear. And they began to go down from that holy mountain to the encampment of iniquity [Fol. 12a, col. 1] of the children of Cain, the murderer, and in this way the fall of the children of Seth took place.

NOTES.--The Book of Adam (ii. 17) says that Yârêd continued to govern the people successfully until the end of the 485th year of his life. At this time Satan and thirty of his devils appeared to Yârêd in the form of handsome men, and called him from the Cave of Treasures. He came out to them, and thought they were strangers, and asked them who they were. In answer,

Satan told him that he was Adam, and that among his companions were Abel, Seth, Enos, Cainan, and other kinsmen of Yârêd. He invited Yârêd to come with him, and live with him in the garden which God had given him, and at length Yârêd was persuaded to leave the Cave and go with him. When they arrived at the top of the mountain of the sons of Cain, Satan pretended that he had left a garment for Yârêd by the Cave, and sent one of his devils back to fetch it, telling him at the same time to extinguish the lamp which was burning in the Cave near Adam's body. Satan and Yârêd rested by a fountain, and food was brought out to them by the sons and daughters of Cain, but Yârêd refused to eat or drink. Satan entreated him to put aside his sadness, and to do as he was going to do. Thereupon Satan and five of his devils each seized a woman and committed fornication with her, and on seeing this exhibition of iniquity Yârêd burst into tears and began to pray to God to be delivered from that place. When he began to pray the devils took to flight, and God sent an angel, who brought him back to his holy mountain. When he returned to the Cave his people told him that the lamp had been extinguished, and that the bodies of the Patriarchs had been scattered about, and that voices had come from them. On entering the Cave a voice came to him from Adam's body, and warned him to beware of Satan and his wiles, and told him to relight the lamp from the fire on the altar at which Adam had ministered. The lamp was relighted at the end of the 450th year of Yârêd's life. Eighty years later his people began to go down to the children of Cain, and to mingle with their women.

AND IN THE FORTIETH YEAR OF YÂRÊD THE FIRST THOUSAND YEARS, FROM ADAM TO YÂRÊD, CAME TO AN END.

And in these years the handicraftsmen of sin, and the disciples of Satan, appeared, for he was their teacher, and he entered in and dwelt in them, and he poured into them the spirit of the operation of error, through which the fall of the children of Seth was to take place.

THE SECOND THOUSAND YEARS: YÂRÊD TO THE FLOOD

OF THE TRANSMISSION OF THE ART OF PLAYING THE HARP, THAT IS TO SAY, OF MUSIC, AND SINGING AND DANCING

YÔBÂL (Jubal) and Tôbalkîn (Tubal-Cain), the two brethren, the sons of Lamech, the blind man, who killed Cain, invented and made all kinds of instruments of music. Jôbâl made reed instruments, and harps, and flutes, and whistles, and the devils went and dwelt inside them. When men blew into the pipes, the devils sang inside them, and sent out sounds from inside them. Tôbalkîn made [Fol. 12a, col. 2] cymbals, and sistra, and tambourines (or drums). And lasciviousness and fornication increased among the children of Cain, and they had nothing to occupy them except fornication--now they had no obligation [to pay] tribute, and they had neither prince nor governor--and eating, and drinking, and lasciviousness, and drunkenness, and dancing and singing to instruments of music, and the wanton sportings of the devils, and the laughter which affordeth pleasure to the devils, and the sounds of the furious lust of men neighing after women. And Satan, finding [his] opportunity in this work of error, rejoiced greatly, because thereby he could compel the sons of Seth to come down from that holy mountain. There they had been made to occupy the place of that army [of angels] that fell [with Satan], there they were beloved by God, there they were held in honour by the angels, and were called "sons of God," even as the blessed David saith in the psalm, "I have said [Fol. 12b, col. 1], Ye are gods, and all of you sons of the Most High." (Ps. lxxxii. 6.)

Meanwhile fornication reigned among the daughters of Cain, and without shame [several] women would run after one man. And one man would attack another, and they committed fornication in the presence of each other shamelessly.   *   *   *   For all the devils were gathered together in that camp of Cain, and unclean spirits entered into the women, and took possession of them. The old women were more lascivious than the maidens, fathers and sons defiled themselves with their mothers and sisters, sons respected not even their own fathers, and fathers made no distinction between their sons [and other men]. And Satan had been made ruler (or prince) of that camp [Fol. 12b, col. 2]. And when the men and women were stirred up to lascivious frenzy by the devilish playing of the reeds which emitted musical sounds, and by the harps which the men played through the operation of the power of the devils, and by the sounds of the tambourines and of the sistra which were beaten and rattled through the agency of evil spirits, the sounds of their laughter were heard in the air above them, and ascended to that holy mountain.

And when the children of Seth heard the noise, and uproar, and shouts of laughter in the camp of the children of Cain, about one hundred of them who were mighty men of war gathered together, and set their faces to go down to the camp of the children of Cain. When Yârêd heard their words and knew their intention, he became sorely afflicted, and he sent and called them to him, and said unto them, "By the holy blood of Abel, I will have you swear that not one of you shall go down from this holy mountain. Remember ye [Fol. 13a, col. 1] the oaths which our fathers Seth, and Ânôsh, and Kainân, and Mahlâlâîl made you to swear." And Enoch also said unto them, "Hearken, O ye children of Seth, no man who shall transgress the commandment of Yârêd, and [break] the oaths of our fathers, and go down from this mountain, shall never again ascend it." But the children of Seth would neither hearken to the commandment of Yârêd, nor to the words of Enoch, and they dared to transgress the commandment, and those hundred men, who were mighty men of war, went down [to the camp of Cain]. And when they saw that the daughters of Cain were beautiful in form and that they were naked and unashamed, the children of Seth became inflamed with the fire of lust. And when the daughters of Cain saw the goodliness of the children of Seth, they gripped them like ravening beasts and defiled their bodies. And the children of Seth slew their souls by fornication with the daughters of Cain. And when the children of Seth wished to go up [again] to that holy mountain [Fol. 13a, col. 2], after they had come down and fallen, the stones of that holy mountain became fire in their sight, and having defiled their souls with the fire of fomication, God did not permit them to ascend to that holy place. And, moreover, very many others made bold and went down after them, and they, too, fell.

NOTES.--This story is told at great length in the Book of Adam (ii. 20). Satan appeared in the form of one Gunnun and taught him to make horns and trumpets, stringed instruments, cymbals, psalteries, lyres, harps and flutes. Into these Satan himself entered, and made the music which came from them. Gunnun made corn spirit, and established drinking booths, in which men assembled and drank and ate fruit. Then Satan taught Gunnun to make weapons of war out of iron, and when men were drunk they killed each other with them. Next Satan taught men how to dye their garments crimson and purple, and they arrayed themselves in gaudy attire, and began to race their horses. Little by little the children of Seth began to wish to join the sons of Cain, and when the devils had shown them a way down the mountain, one hundred of them went down to the plain, and were led astray by the women whose hands and feet were stained with bright colours and whose faces had tattoo marks on them. When the Sethites tried to return to the top of the mountain, the stones turned into coals of fire, and they could not pass over them. Company after company of the children of Seth went down to the plain, and at length only Yârêd and a few others remained on the mountain. The Ethiopic Book of Enoch (see the translations by Archbishop Lawrence, Oxford, 1838, by Dillmann, Leipzig, 1853, and Canon Charles, Oxford, 1893) supplies interesting details about the fall of the children of Seth. The leaders of those who went down from Ardis on Mount Hermon were Semyâzâ, the commander-in-chief, Urâkîbarâmê'êl, Kôkabî'êl, Tâmi'êl, Râmu'êl, Dân'êl, Zakîlô, Sarâkuyâl, Asâ'êl, Armârôs, Batraal, 'Anânî, Zakêbê, Samsâwe'êl, Sarta'êl, Tur'êl, Yomyâ'êl, and 'Azâzyâl. Each of these was over a company of ten. The names of two of the dekarchs of the 200 angels are omitted. These angels took to themselves wives, and taught them the use of spells and enchantments, and the use of plants and trees [for medicinal purposes ?]. The daughters of Cain conceived, and a tradition in the Kebra Nagast says that the children were so large that they could not be born in the ordinary way, but had to be removed from their mothers by the umbilicus.[3] These children grew up and became giants 3,000 cubits in height, and when they had devoured all the provisions which their neighbours had collected, they began to fight against men and to eat them, and at length they ate the flesh and drank the blood of each other. Concerning these giants, the Book of Enoch (chapter xv) says, "Now, the giants, who were produced from the spirits and the flesh, shall be called evil spirits on earth, and their habitation shall be on the earth. Evil spirits shall proceed from their bodies. . . . And the spirits of the giants shall consume, and persecute, and lay waste, and fight and work destruction on the earth and afflict [men]. They shall neither eat food of any kind, nor suffer thirst, and they shall remain invisible. And these spirits shall attack the children of men and women, for from them have they come forth." The wickedness of these giants became so great that the earth complained [to God]. At this time 'Azâz'êl taught men the art of working in metals, and the use of stibium, or eye-paint, and the art of dyeing stuffs in bright colours. ´Amêzârâk taught enchantments (i.e. magic) and the knowledge of herbs; ´Armârôs taught how spells were to be broken; Barak`âl taught astrology; Kôkab´êl taught the knowledge of signs; Tem´êl taught astronomy; and ´Asrâdêl taught concerning the moon [Book of Enoch, chapter viii.] The originals of these Seven Sages were probably the Seven Wise Men who were revered by the Babylonians.

And when Yârêd had lived nine hundred and sixty years, and the day of his departure approached, and came nigh, and arrived, all the Patriarchs gathered themselves together and came unto him, viz. Enoch, his first-born, and Methuselah, and Lamech, and Noah, they and their wives and their children, and were blessed by him. And he prayed over them, and said unto them, "I will make you to swear by the holy blood of Abel that you will not go down from this holy mountain; for I know that God will not allow you to remain very much longer in this holy country. Inasmuch as [Fol. 13b, col. 1] ye have transgressed the commandment of your fathers, ye shall surely be cast out into that outer country, and ye shall no longer have your habitation on the skirts [of the mountain] of Paradise. And take ye good heed to this. Let him that is among you who shall go forth from that holy country take with him the body of our father Adam, and the offerings [of gold, frankincense, and myrrh] that are in the Cave of Treasures, and let him carry away and deposit the body in the place wherein he shall be commanded by God to set it down. And thou, my son Enoch, depart thou not from before the body of Adam, but minister before God purely and holily all the days of thy life." And Yârêd died, [being] nine hundred and sixty-two years old, on the thirteenth day of the month of Îyâr (May), on the day of the Eve of the Sabbath (Friday), at sunset, in the three hundred and sixty-sixth year of the life of Noah. And Enoch his son embalmed him, and buried him in the Cave of Treasures; and they made mourning for him forty days.

NOTES.--The Book of the Bee says that Yârêd was 962 years old when he died, and that he begot Enoch when he was 162 years old. The Book of Adam says that he was 989 years old when he died, and that he died on Friday, the 12th day of the month of Takhsâs (December) in the 360th year of the life of Noah (ii. 21).

The Rule of Enoch

And Enoch stood up to minister before God in the Cave of Treasures. And the children of Seth turned aside from the right path and willed to go down [to the children of Cain on the plain]. And Enoch and Methuselah, and Lamech and Noah mourned over them. And Enoch had ministered before God for fifty years in the three hundred and [sixty] fifth year of the life of Noah. And when Enoch knew that God was about to remove him [from the earth], he called Methuselah, and Lamech, and Noah, and said unto them, "I know that God is wroth with this generation, and that a pitiless judgment hath been decreed for the people thereof. Ye are the chiefs of this generation and the remnant thereof, for no other man shall be born on this mountain who shall be the chief of the children of his people. But take ye good heed to yourselves, and see that ye minister before God in purity and holiness." And when Enoch had given them his commandment in these words, God removed him to the Land of Life, and to the [Fol. 14a, col. 1] delectable mansions which are round about Paradise, and to that country which is beyond the reach of death. And of all the children of Seth there remained only these three Patriarchs in the "Mountain of the Triumphant Ones," viz. Methuselah, Lamech, and Noah, for all the others had betaken themselves to the encampment of the sons of Cain.

NOTES.--Then Michael, Gabriel, Suriel, and Uriel looked down from heaven, and saw the wickedness which ´Azâz´êl had done in the world, and they heard the appeal which the souls of the dead were making to heaven, and they reported the matter to the Most High. When God heard their words He sent the angel ´Arsyalâlyûr to the son of Lamech, i.e. Noah, with the command, "Hide thyself." No mention is made of Methuselah, who begot Lamech when he was 187 years old, and who lived 969 years, and Lamech, who lived 777 years, and begot Noah in the 182nd year of his age, was passed over in favour of his son. Noah consolidated his position by marrying the daughter of Enoch. The angel revealed to Noah that a flood was about to cover the earth, and told him how to escape from it. Then God commanded Rafa´êl to bind ´Azâz´êl hand and foot, and to thrust him into a dark hole in the desert of Dudâ´êl (a place near Jerusalem ?), and heap stones and rocks upon him. There he was to remain until the Day of judgment, when he would be cast into the fire and consumed. Gabriel was sent to destroy all the children of fornication; and Michael was sent to bind Semyâzâ and the other dekarchs of the children of Seth, and to imprison them under the mountains of the earth for 70 generations, after which time they were to be taken to the abyss of fire and tortured there for ever. Book of Enoch (chapter x).

The Book of the Mysteries of Heaven and Earth, by Abbâ Bakhayla-Mîkâ´êl (ed. Perruchon), says that it was the men who taught man the arts of civilisation, who caused God to bring the Flood on the earth. This work gives the names of these men and describes their inventions thus:--

Pîpîrôs understood the sun, Rûrîdê quarried stones, Zar´êl instituted the month, Pînênê introduced horse-riding (or racing), Gâlê invented the axe, Tîgana invented the shield, Hôrêrî taught men to play musical instruments, Yuebê taught working in iron, Mêgêd taught horse-riding, Negôdî discovered medicinal springs, and made known the planetary hours when the waters were most effective, Gargê made the first corn-grinder, Sêtêr taught men how to mix dough, Gîmêr taught the use of earthenware vessels for food, Zârê taught men to milk animals, Heggê taught men to make roofs, and Tentôreb showed them how to make doors, Sâpêr taught butter-making, Halâgê discovered how to carve wood and stone, Hêder was the first to cultivate trees, Sînô taught house-building, and Tôf invented the potter's craft, Artôrbegâs invented agricultural implements, Sêbêdêgâz introduced the use of kohl (eye-paint, stibium), Zârê invented the brewing of beer, Bêtênêlâdâs invented the oven, Nâfîl taught men to make plantations and gardens, Yârbeh discovered how to fell trees and saw them up, ´Êlyô taught dancing, Pênêmûs invented architecture and writing, ´Agâlêmûn taught the use of beasts in ploughing and how to drive furrows, Kueses invented ploughs and leather whips, ´Akôr discovered bronze (copper ?), certain men taught working in cedar and willow-wood, Wasag and ´Abêregyâ taught men the game of Tâbat, and Nêr and Zabêrêgued taught them to play the games of ´Atâwemâ and ´Akîs, and the games of the circus.]

The Rule of Noah

And when Noah saw that sin had increased in his generation, he preserved himself in virginity for five hundred years. Then God spake unto him and said unto him, "Take unto thee to wife Haykêl, the daughter of Namûs (or Haykêl Namûs), the daughter of Enoch, the brother of Methuselah." And God revealed unto him concerning the Flood which He was making ready to produce, and He spake to him and said unto him) "One hundred and thirty years from this moment I will make a Flood."

NOTES.--The Book of Adam says that Haykêl was the daughter of Abaraz, who was one of the children of the family of Enos, who went into perdition. If this be so, Noah married a woman who was akin to the children of Cain. The Book of the Bee (chapter xx) merely states that Noah's wife was of the children of Seth.

The Building of the Ark

And God said unto Noah, "Make for thyself an ark for the saving of the children of thy house, and build it [in the plain] below [this mountain], in the encampment of the children of Cain, and ye shall cut down the timber for the same [from the trees that are on] this mountain [Fol. 14a, col. 2]. And thus shall be the dimensions thereof. Its length shall be three hundred cubits according to thy cubit, its breadth shall be fifty cubits, and its height thirty cubits; and above it shall be finished off one cubit. And make three storeys in it: the lowermost shall be for wild animals and cattle, the middle one shall be for the birds and feathered fowl, and the topmost shall be for thee and the children of thy house. And make in it cisterns for water and cupboards for food. And make to thyself a striking board of eshkar`a wood which will not rot, three cubits long and a cubit and a half in breadth; and there shall be a hammer of the same kind of wood, and with it thou shalt strike [the board] three times in the day. Once in the morning that the workmen may be gathered together for the work of the ark, and once at midday that they may eat food, and once at sunset so that they may cease from their labour. And when thou strikest the board, and men hear the sound of the blows, and say unto thee, 'What is this that thou doest?' [Fol. 14b, col. 1], thou shalt say unto them, 'God is going to make a flood of waters.'" And Noah did as God commanded him. And there were born unto him three sons within the space of a hundred years, Shem, Ham, and Japhet, and they took unto them wives of the daughters of Methuselah.

NOTES.--According to the Book of the Bee, the storeys were to have boards and projecting ledges, each board being one cubit long and one span broad. The wood used was either box or teak, and the Ark was pitched within and without. The Book of Adam (iii. 2) says that each storey was 10 cubits high. The first was for lions and other animals, and ostriches, the second was for birds and reptiles, and the third for Noah and his sons, Shem, Ham, and Japhet, and their wives. The cisterns were to be lined with lead, inside and out. Noah begot his sons during the hundred years in which he was building the Ark; during these years he ate no animal food, and he wore the same pair of sandals, which did not wear out, and the same apparel and head cloth, and carried the same staff. His hair neither increased nor diminished. His sons married daughters of Methuselah.

The Death of Lamech

And when Lamech had lived seven hundred and seventy years, he died during the lifetime of Methuselah, his father, forty years before the Flood, on the twenty-first day of the month of Îlûl (September), on the first day of the week (Sunday), in the sixty-eighth year of the life of Shem, the firstborn of Noah. And Noah his firstborn embalmed him, and Methuselah his father swathed him for burial, and they buried him in the Cave of Treasures, and mourned for him forty days.

NOTES.--The Book of Adam says that Lamech was 553 years old when he died, but the Book of the Bee gives his age as 774 or 777 years; the former work says that Lamech died seven years before the Flood.

The Rule of Methuselah and Noah

And Methuselah and Noah remained alone on the mountain, for all the children of Seth had gone down from the skirts of the mountain of Paradise to the plain where the children of Cain lived [Fol. 14b, col. 2]. And men, the children of Seth, had intercourse with the daughters of Cain, who conceived of them, and brought forth men, giants and the sons of giants, who were like unto towers. Now because of this certain ancient writers have fallen into error, and have written, "The angels came down from heaven, and had intercourse with men, and by them these famous giants have been produced." But this is not true, for those who have written in this manner did not understand [the facts]. Behold, O my brother-readers, and know ye that it is not in the nature of beings of the spirit to beget, neither is it in the nature of the devils--who are unclean beings, and workers of wickedness, and lovers of adultery--to beget, because there are neither males nor females among them. And since the time when the angels fell, not another angel has been added to their number. And if the devils were able to have intercourse with women they would not leave unravished a single virgin [Fol. 15a, col. 1] in all the race of the children of men.

The Death of Methuselah

And when Methuselah had lived nine hundred and sixty-nine years, and the day of his departure had drawn nigh, Noah, and Shem, and Ham, and Japhet, and their wives, came unto him. Now of all the posterity of Seth who had not betaken themselves down to the plain, only these eight souls were left, viz. Noah, Shem, Ham, Japhet, and their wives; for no children were born to them before the Flood. And when these gathered themselves together to Methuselah, and they had been blessed by him, he embraced them, and kissed them sorrowfully, and wept over the fall of the children of Seth. And he said unto them, "Of all the tribes and families of your fathers, this remnant [consisting] of eight souls [Fol. 15a, col. 2] alone is left. May the Lord God of our fathers bless you! The Lord God who formed our father Adam and Eve by themselves (and they were fruitful, and multiplied, and the whole of the blessed land which was round about Paradise was filled with their progeny), shall make you to be fruitful, and to multiply, and the whole earth shall be filled with you. He shall save you from the terrible wrath which hath been decreed against this rebellious generation, and He shall be with you, and He shall protect you. And the gift which was given by God unto our father Adam shall go forth with you from this holy country. And these three measures of the wheat of blessings which God gave unto your father Adam shall serve as leaven, and shall be kneaded into your seed, and into the seed of your children, that is to say, Royalty, Priesthood, and Prophecy.

"Hearken thou, Noah, thou blessed of the Lord. Behold [Fol. 15b, col. 1], I am going forth from this world, like all my fathers, but thou and thy children shall be saved. And thou shalt do everything which I am command-ing you to do this day, [for] God will make the Flood. When I die, embalm my body, and bury me in the Cave of Treasures with my fathers. Take thy wife, and thy sons, and the wives of thy sons, and get thee down from this holy mountain. And take with thee the body of our father Adam, and these three offerings, gold, and myrrh, and frankincense; set the body of Adam in the middle of the Ark, and lay these offerings upon him. Thou and thy sons shall occupy the eastern part of the Ark, and thy wife and thy son's wives shall occupy the western part thereof; thy wives shall not pass over to you, and ye shall not pass over to them. Ye shall neither eat nor drink with them, and ye shall have no intercourse whatsoever with them until ye go forth [Fol. 15b, col. 2] from the Ark. Now this generation hath provoked God to wrath, and He will neither permit them to be neighbours of [those who are in] Paradise, nor to praise Him with the angels.

"And when the waters of the Flood have subsided from the face of the earth, and ye go forth from the Ark, and ye take up your abode in that land, thou, O Noah, the blessed of the Lord, shall not depart from the Ark, from the body of our father Adam, but minister thou before God in the Ark purely and holily all the days of thy life. And these offerings shall be placed in the east. And command thou Shem, thy firstborn, to take up with him, after thy death, the body of our father Adam, and to carry it and deposit it in the middle of the earth. And let him establish there a man from among his descendants who shall minister there. And he shall be one who is set apart (nezîrâ) all the days of his life. He shall not take a wife, he shall not shed blood, he shall not offer up [Fol. 16a, col. 1] these offerings of wild animals and feathered fowl; but he shall offer unto God bread and wine, for by these redemption shall be made for Adam and all his posterity. And the Angel of God shall go before him, and he shall show him the place where the middle of the earth is situated. And the apparel of him that shall stand up there to minister before the body of Adam shall be the skins of wild animals. He shall not shave off the hair of his head, and he shall not cut his nails, but he shall remain alone (in his natural state ?) because he is the priest of God, the Most High."

NOTES.--According to the Book of Adam, (iii. 5), Shem was to appoint Melchisedek (see Gen. xiv. 18-24; Heb., chapter vii.), the son of Kainân, and grandson of Arphaxad, to be the priest of the Most High; and he was to stand and minister on the mountain which is in the middle of the earth. He was to wear a garment of skin, and have a leather girdle about his loins, and his apparel was to be humble and without ornament.

And when Methuselah had commanded Noah [to do] all these things, he died with tears in his eyes, and sorrow in his heart. He was nine hundred and sixty-nine years old when he died, on the fourteenth day of the month Âdhâr (March), on the first day of the week (Sunday), in the seventy-ninth year [Fol. 16a, col. 2] of the life of Shem, the son of Noah. And Noah, his grandson, embalmed the body of Methuselah with myrrh, and cassia, and stakte, and Noah and his sons buried him in the Cave of Treasures; and they and their wives made mourning for him forty days.

And when the days of his mourning had passed, Noah went into the Cave of Treasures, and embraced and kissed the holy bodies of Seth, and Ânôsh, and Kainân, and Mahlâlâîl, and Yârêd, and Methuselah, and Lamech his father, and he was greatly moved and tears gushed from his eyes. And

Noah carried the body of our father Adam, and [the body of] Eve, and his firstborn Shem carried the gold, and Ham carried the myrrh, and Japhet the frankincense, and they went forth from the Cave of Treasures. [The Book of Adam does not mention Eve.]. And as they were coming down from that holy mountain they were smitten sorely with grief: and they wept in agony because they were to be deprived of that [Fol. 16b, col. 1] holy place, and the habitation of their fathers. And weeping painfully, and wailing sorrowfully, and enveloped in gloom, they said,

"Remain in peace! O holy Paradise, thou habitation of our father Adam.
He went forth from thee alive, but stripped [of glory] and naked.
And behold, at his death he was deprived of thy nearness.
He and his progeny were cast out into exile in that land of curses, to pass their days there in pain, and sicknesses, and in labour, and in weariness, and in trouble.
Remain in peace, O Cave of Treasures!
Remain in peace, O habitation and inheritance of our Fathers!
Remain ye in peace, O our Fathers and Patriarchs!
Pray ye for us, O ye who live in the dust, ye friends and beloved ones of the Living God.
Pray ye for the remnant of your posterity which is left.
O ye who have propitiated God, make supplication unto Him on our behalf in your prayers. [Fol. 16b, col. 2.]
Remain in peace, O Ânôsh!
Remain ye in peace, O ye ministers of God, Kainân, and Mahlâlâîl, and Yârêd, and Methuselah, and Lamech, and Enoch! Cry out in sorrow on our behalf.
Remain in peace, O Haven and Asylum of the Angels!
O ye our Fathers, cry out in sorrow on our behalf, because ye will be deprived of our society!
And we will cry out in sorrow, because we are cast out into a bare land, for our habitation will be with the wild beasts."

And as they were coming down from that holy mountain, they kissed the stones thereof, and embraced the delectable trees thereof. And in this wise they came down, and they wept with great sorrow, and shed scalding (or bitter) tears, and suffering sorely they descended to the plain. And Noah went into the Ark, and deposited the body of Adam in the middle thereof, and he placed these [Fol. 17a, col. 1] offerings upon it.

Now in the year wherein Noah went into the Ark THE SECOND THOUSAND YEARS OF THE POSTERITY OF ADAM TO THE TIME OF THE FLOOD CAME TO AN END, according to what the Seventy Wise Writers have told us.

NOTES.--The Book of Adam (iii. 6) says that when Noah and his sons were carrying the body of Adam out of the Cave, the bodies of the other Patriarchs cried out, and asked the body of Adam if they were to be separated from it. Adam replied that he must leave the holy mountain, and told them that he knew God would bring their bodies together again on another occasion, and bade them wait patiently. Adam asked God to allow the lighted lamp to remain with the bodies in the Cave, until the resurrection. This God did, and then He closed the Cave until the day of the resurrection. Noah and his sons marvelled greatly when they heard the bodies of the Patriarchs talking together in the Cave. Having carried away the body of Adam and the gold, myrrh and frankincense, they returned to the mountain, intending to enter the Cave once agaln; they sought carefully, but could not find the Cave, and then they knew that God had sealed it, and had hidden it from them, so that they might never dwell therein again.

THE THIRD THOUSAND YEARS: FROM THE FLOOD TO THE REIGN OF REU

Noah's entry into the Ark

THE entrance of Noah into the Ark took place on the day of the eve of the Sabbath (Friday), on the seventeenth day of the blessed month of Îyâr (May). On the Friday, in the morning (i.e. the third hour) the beasts and the cattle went into the lowermost storey; and at midday all the feathered fowl and all the reptiles went into the middle storey; and at sunset Noah and his sons went into the Ark, on the east side of [the third storey], and his wife and the wives of his sons went to the west side. And the body of Adam was deposited in the middle of the Ark, wherein also all the mysteries of the Church were deposited. Thus women in church shall be on the west [side] [Fol. 17a, col. 2], and men on the east [side], so that the men may not see the faces of the women, and the women may not see the faces of the men. Thus also was it in the Ark; the women were on the west [side], and the men on the east [side], and the body of our father Adam was placed between [them] like a raised stand (or throne). And as quietness reigneth in the Church between men and women, so also peace reigned in the Ark between the wild beasts, and the feathered fowl, and the creeping things (or reptiles). And as kings, and judges, and rich men, and poor men, and governors, and sick men, and beggars, live in concord, that is to say, in a general bond of peace, so also was it in the Ark. For lions, and panthers, and savage beasts of prey lived in peace and harmony with the cattle; and the beasts that were fierce and strong lived in peace with those that were timid and weak; and the lion with the ox, and the wolf with the lamb, and the lion's whelp [Fol. 17b, col. 1] with the calf, and the serpent with the dove, and the hawk with the sparrow.

The Flood

And when Noah and his sons had gone into the Ark, and his wife and the wives of his sons, on the seventeenth day of the month of Îyâr (May), at sunset, the door of the Ark was shut fast, and Noah and his sons in captivity in the darkness. And as soon as the door of the Ark was shut, the floodgates of the heavens were opened, and the foundations of the earth were rent asunder, and Ocean, that great sea which surroundeth the whole world, poured forth its floods. And whilst the floodgates of heaven were open, and the foundations of the earth were rent asunder, the storehouses of the winds burst their bolts, and storm and whirlwinds swept forth, and Ocean roared and hurled its floods upon the earth. And the children of Seth, who had besmirched themselves in the mire of fornication, ran to the door of the Ark, and entreated Noah to open to them the door of the Ark. And when they saw the water floods which were swirling about them and engulfing [Fol. 17b, col. 2] them on all sides, they were in great tribulation, and they tried to climb up the mountains of Paradise, but were unable to do so. Now the Ark was closed and sealed, and the Angel of the Lord stood over one side of it that he might act as the pilot thereof. And when the floods of waters mastered the children of Seth, and they began to drown in their great and mighty waves--then was fulfilled that which David spake concerning them, saying, "I said, Ye are gods, and all of you sons of the Most High. (Ps. lxxxii. 6.) But since ye have done this, and ye have loved the fornication of the daughters of Cain, like them ye shall perish, and even as they did so shall ye die."

And when the Ark was lifted up from the earth by the mighty strength of the waters, all the children of men, and the wild beasts, and the feathered fowl, and the cattle, and the creeping things, and everything [living] on the face of the earth was drowned. And the waters [Fol. 18a, col. 1] of the Flood mounted up above all the tops of the high mountains fifteen cubits [variants, 25, 50 cubits], according to the measure of the Spirit. [The cubit of the Holy Ghost = 3 ordinary cubits.] And the flood waxed strong, and the waters thereof lifted up the Ark until it reached the skirts [of the mountain] of Paradise. And as the flood had been blessed by Paradise (i.e. had been made holy), it bowed its head, and kissed the skirts of Paradise and turned itself back to destroy the whole earth. And the Ark flew on the wings of the wind over the waters of the flood from east to west, and from north to south, and it marked out [by its path] a cross on the waters. And the Ark flew about for one hundred and fifty days, and it came to rest on the mountains of Kardô (i.e. Ararat, the Jabal al-Jûdî of the Arabs, near Jazîrat ibn ʿUmar) in the seventh month, that is to say, in the First Teshrî (October) on the seventeenth day thereof. And God commanded the waters, and they became separated from each other. The celestial waters were taken up, and ascended to their own place above [Fol. 18a, col. 2] the heavens, whence they came. The waters which had risen up from the earth returned to the lowermost abyss [under the earth]; and those which belonged to the Ocean [which surroundeth the whole world] returned to the innermost parts thereof. And the waters which had been on the earth, and had been assigned to it by the Divine Nod for the needs thereof from the beginning, remained upon it.

And the waters diminished little by little until the tenth month, which is Shebât (February), and on the first day thereof the tops of the mountains appeared. And, forty days later, on the tenth day of the month of Âdhâr (March), Noah opened the east window of the Ark, and sent forth a raven to bring back tidings; and the raven departed and did not return. And after the waters had diminished a little more from the earth, Noah sent forth a dove; and it found no place to rest, and it returned to Noah to the Ark. And after seven days he sent forth another dove, and it returned to him, carrying in its beak an olive leaf. Now the dove figureth for us the Two Covenants. In the First Covenant [Fol. 18b, col. 1] the spirit which spake by the Prophets did not find a place of rest among that rebellious people (i.e. the Jews); and in the Second Covenant it rested on the peoples through the waters of baptism.

NOTES.--The above description of the Flood agrees substantially with that given in the Book of Adam (chapters ix and x), and in the Book of the Bee (chapter xx).

Noah leaves the Ark

And in the six hundred and first year of the life of Noah, on the first day of the month of Nîsân (April) the waters had dried up from the face of the earth. And in the second month, which is Îyâr (May), wherein Noah went into the Ark on the twenty-seventh day, on the holy first day of the week (Sunday), their going forth took place; and he and his wife went forth, and his sons and their wives went with them. Now, when they went into the Ark they went in in separate companies, Noah and his sons [in one company], and his wife and their wives in another company; and the men did not know the women until they went forth from the Ark. And all the wild beasts, and all the cattle, and all the feathered fowl, and all the creeping things went forth from the Ark on the first day of the week.

Noah founds Themânôn, the city of the "Eight"

And when they had gone forth Noah began work on the ground [Fol. 18b, col. 2], and they built a city and called the name thereof "Themânôn" (i.e. "Eight"), after the name of the eight souls who had gone forth from the Ark. And Noah built an altar, and offered up upon it an offering of beasts that were clean and feathered fowl. And God was appeased by the offering of Noah, and he established with him an everlasting covenant, and swore an oath, saying, "I will never again make a Flood." He took away the arrow of wrath from the bow which is in the clouds, and he stripped from it the string of anger, and spread it out (i.e. unbent it) in the clouds. For formerly, when the bow was bent in the firmament against that generation of the children of Cain, the murderer, they used to see the arrow of wrath placed in position on the string of anger, but after the Flood they did not see the arrow on the string.

NOTE.--According to the Book of Adam (iii. 11), the waters dried up in the 607th year of the life of Noah. The altar on which Noah sacrificed was that on which Adam, Cain, and Abel had laid their offerings; it had been damaged by the Flood, but Noah rebuilt it. The city of Themânôn is îdentified with Sûbhâ (i.e. Nisîbis) in the Book of the Bee (chapter xx), but this is a false identification. The "City of Eight," Themânôn, is not to be identified with the τὸ Θομάνων {Greek: tò Đománwn} of Theophylact Simocatta (vol. ii. chap. 10, p. 86), which lay on the right bank of the Tigris near Hisn Kêfâ, but with the Sûk Thamânîn of the Arab geographers, which lay at a distance of one day's journey from Jazîrat ibn `Umar. It was situated high up in the mountains, and Khusraw Anôsharwân used to encamp there during the heats of summer. Near Burzmihrân, and between Jazîrat ibn `Umar and Thamânôn was Dêr Abbûn, which, according to Yâkût, contained the tomb of Noah. It is interesting to note that the Arabs call Noah's city Sûk Thamânîn (i.e. "Market of the Eighty") and not "Market of the Eight." For further details see Hoffmann, G., Auszüge aus syrischen Akten, page 174.

The Vineyard of Noah

And when they had gone forth from the Ark, they sowed seed and planted a vineyard; and they pressed out new wine. And Noah drew nigh, and drank some of it, and immediately he had drunk of it [Fol. 19a, col. 1] he became drunk. And having fallen asleep, his shame was seen, and his son Ham saw the nakedness of his father, and did not cover it; but he laughed at him and made a mock of him, and he ran and called his brethren that they also might make a mock of their father. And when Shem and Japhet heard of it they were dismayed exceedingly. And they rose up, and took a cloak, and walked backwards with their faces turned away that they might not see the nakedness of their father. And they cast the cloak over him and covered him. And when Noah woke up from the sleep of his wine, his wife told him about everything that had happened, and he also within himself knew what had happened to him. And Noah was exceedingly angry with his son Ham, and he said, "Cursed be Canaan; he shall be a servant of servants to his brethren."

Why, since the whole of the folly was Ham's, was Canaan cursed, except that, when the youth grew up [Fol. 19a, col. 2], and attained the full measure of his understanding, Satan entered into him, and became to him a teacher of sin? And he renewed the work of the house of Cain, the murderer. He constructed and made reed instruments and harps, and the fiends and the devils went unto them and dwelt therein. And immediately wind was blown through them (the reeds), the devils sang inside them, and sent forth loud sounds; and when men struck the harps the devils became operative inside them. And when Noah heard that Canaan had done this, he was grieved sorely, because the work of error, through which the fall of the children of Seth had taken place, was renewed. For by means of singing, and lewd play, and the mad lasciviousness of the children of Cain, Satan had cast down the mighty men, the "sons of God," into fornication. And through the music of reed pipes and harps sin had multiplied [Fol. 19b, col. 1] among the former generations until, at length, God became wroth and made the Flood. And Canaan was cursed because he had dared to do this, and his seed became a servant of servants, that is to say, to the Egyptians, and the Cushites, and the Mûsâyê (Mysians), [and the Indians, and all the Ethiopians, whose skins are black]. And because Ham had dared to make a mock of his father he was called "vile" (or "lascivious") all the days of his life.

Now Noah in his lying down in sleep, having drunk wine, symbolizeth the Cross of Christ, as the blessed man David singeth in his Psalm concerning him, saying, "Wake up, Lord, like a sleeping man, and like a man whom wine hath overcome." [Compare Psalm xlv. 23 {sic, Psalm xliv. 23}; lxxviii. 65.] Let the heretics who say "God was crucified" hold their peace. Here David calleth him "Lord," even as Peter the Apostle said, "This Jesus, whom ye crucified, hath God made Lord and Messiah (Christ)." (Compare Acts v. 30, 31.] He did not say "God" (Allâhâ), but "Lord" (Mâryâ), thus [Fol. 19b, col. 2] making known concerning the unity (or oneness) of the Two Persons who were united in one sonship. Now when Noah woke up from his sleep he cursed Canaan, and reduced his seed to slavery, and scattered his seed among the nations. And when our Lord rose from the dead He cursed the Jews, and scattered them among the nations. Now the seed of Canaan, as I have already said, are the Egyptians, and behold, they are scattered over the whole earth, and have been made servants of servants. And of what kind is this slavery of slavery? Behold, the Egyptians go round about all over the earth carrying loads on their backs (literally, necks). Now, men who are not fettered under the yoke of slavery, when despatched by their masters on journeys, do not march on their feet and carry loads, but they ride upon beasts in an honourable manner, like their masters. The seed of Ham are the Egyptians who carry loads, and they march [Fol. 20a, col. 1] on the roads with their backs and necks breaking under their loads, and they wander round to the doors of the children of their brethren. The seed of Ham was reduced, through the folly of Canaan, to suffer this penalty, that is, to become servants even to servants.

NOTE.--The Book of the Bee (chapter xx) says concerning the cursing of Ham, "The reason why he (Noah) cursed Canaan, who was not as yet born, nor had sinned, was because Ham had been saved with him in the Ark from the waters of the Flood, and had with his father received the divine blessing, and also because the arts of sin--I mean music and dancing and all other hateful things--were about to be revived by his posterity, for the art of music proceeded from the seed of Canaan." The same work adds, "After the Flood a son was born to Noah, and he called his name Yônatôn; and he provided him with gifts and sent him to the fire of the sun, to the east." The Book of Adam (iii. 13), merely states that Noah married another wife, who bore him seven children, and that he continued to dwell on that mountain until the end of his days.

The Death of Noah

And Noah lived three hundred and fifty years after he came forth from the Ark. And when he was sick unto death, Shem, and Ham, and Japhet, and Arpakhshar (Arphaxad), and Shâlah (Salah) gathered together unto him. And Noah called Shem, his firstborn, and said unto him privily, "Take heed, my son Shem, unto what I say unto thee this day. When I am dead, go into the Ark, wherein thou hast been saved, and bring out the body of our father Adam, and let no man have knowledge of what thou doest. And take with thee from this place provision for the way, bread and wine, and take with thee Melchisedek, the son of Mâlâkh [Fol. 20a, col. 2], because him hath God chosen from among all your descendants that he may minister before Him in respect of the body of our father Adam. And take the body and place it in the centre of the earth, and make Melchisedek to sit down there. And the Angel of God shall go before you, and shall show you the way wherein ye shall go, and also the place wherein the body of Adam shall be deposited, which is, indeed, the centre of the earth. There the four quarters of the earth embrace each other. For when God made the earth His power went before it, and the earth, from [its] four quarters, ran after it, like the winds and the swift breezes, and there (i.e. in the centre of the earth) His power stood still and was motionless. There shall redemption be made for Adam, and for all his posterity. Now this story, or mystery, was handed down to us from Adam in all generations [Fol. 20b, col. 1]. Adam commanded Seth, and Seth commanded Ânôsh (Enos), and Ânôsh commanded Kainân (Cainan), and Kainân commanded Mahlâlâîl, and Mahlâlâîl commanded Yârêd, and Yârêd commanded Enoch, and Enoch commanded Methuselah, and Methuselah commanded Lamech; and behold, I command thee this day. And take heed that this story is never mentioned again in all your generations. Get thee up, and take the body of Adam, and deposit it secretly in the place which God shall show thee until the day of redemption." And when Noah had given all these commands unto his son Shem, he died, [being] nine hundred and fifty years old, in the month of Îyâr (May), on the second day thereof, at the second hour of the first day of the week (Sunday). And Shem his son embalmed him, and buried him in the city which he had built (i.e. Themânôn), and they made a mourning for him forty days.

NOTES.--According to the Book of the Bee, Noah died on the fourth day of the week (Wednesday), on the second day of the month of Nîsân (April), at the second hour of the day. The Book of Adam says that he was buried on the mountain on which the Ark rested. The same authority states (iii. chapter xiv) that the Ark was closed during the days of Noah, but that Noah went into it every evening to light the lamp which he had made, and which burned before the body of Adam. It is also stated that during his dying speech Noah indicated to each of his sons which part of the earth he was to dwell with his posterity. The territory of Shem extended from Jerusalem eastwards as far as India, and southwards as far as the mountains which divided Egypt from the land of the Philistines. It included Mount Zion, Mount Sinai, and the Garden of Eden. Ham's territory extended from Aris towards the south, as far as Fardundan and Gadariun, and also to the borders of the west. Japhet's portion was very large, and extended from the angle of the west to Damatha in the south, and all the north as far as Aris. Canaan, a descendant of Ham, had seven sons, and he seized seven of the great cities of Shem, and set these sons over them; and he doubled the size of his own portion. Later, God gave these cities back to the children of Shem, and blotted out Canaan's posterity, Kebra Nagast (chapter xii).

The Departure of Shem with the body of Adam

And after the death of Noah Shem did as his father had commanded him. And he went into [Fol. 20b, col. 2] the Ark by night, and brought out the body of Adam therefrom, and he sealed the Ark with his father's seal, and no man perceived [what he had done]. And he called Ham and Japhet, and said unto them, "My brethren, my father commanded me to go up and travel over the earth, even to the sea (i.e. the Mediterranean), and I am to see what the rivers are like, and then return unto you. And behold, my wife and the children of my house are with you (i.e. in your care); let your eyes be upon them." And his brethren said unto him, "Take with thee a company of men from the camp, for the land is a desert waste, and is shorn of inhabitants, and there are wild beasts therein." And Shem said unto them, "The Angel of the Lord shall go up with me, and he shall save me from every evil thing"; and his brethren said unto him, "Go in peace, and may the Lord God of our Fathers be with thee." And Shem said unto Mâlâkh (the brother of Shâlâh (Salah), the son of [Cainan] and [grand]son of Arphaxad), the father of Melchisedek, and Yôzadhâk, his mother, "Give ye me Melchisedek [Fol. 21a, col. 1], that he may go up with me, and be a consolation for me on the road." And Mâlâkh and Yôzadhâk, his mother, said unto Shem, "Take [him] and go in peace." And Shem gave commands unto his brethren, and said unto them, "My brethren, my father made me swear that neither I, nor any of your descendants, should go into the Ark," and he sealed the Ark with his seal, and said unto them, "Let no man go near it."

Shem carries the body of Adam to Golgotha

And Shem took the body of Adam and Melchisedek, and went forth by night from among his people, and behold, the Angel of the Lord, who was going before them, appeared unto them. And their journey was very speedy, because the Angel of the Lord strengthened them until they arrived at that place. And when they arrived at Gâghûltâ (Golgotha), which is the centre of the earth, the Angel of the Lord showed Shem the place [for the body of Adam]. And when Shem had deposited the body of our father Adam upon that place [Fol. 21a, col. 2], the four quarters [of the earth] separated themselves from each other, and the earth opened itself in the form of a cross, and Shem and Melchisedek deposited the body of Adam there (i.e. in the cavity). And as soon as they had laid it therein, the four quarters [of the earth] drew quickly together, and enclosed the body of our father Adam, and the door of the created world was shut fast. And that place was called "Karkaphtâ " (i.e. "Skull"), because the head of all the children of men was deposited there. And it was called "Gâghûltâ," because it was round [like the head], and "Resîphtâ " (i.e. a trodden-down thing), because the head of the accursed serpent, that is to say, Satan, was crushed there, and "Gefîftâ " (Gabbatha), because all the nations were to be gathered together to it.

NOTES.--The Book of the Bee devotes a chapter (xxi) to Melchisedek, and says that neither the father nor mother of this Melchisedek were written down in the genealogies; not that he had no natural parents, but that they were not written down. The greater number of the doctors say that he was of the sect of Canaan, whom Noah cursed. In the Book of Chronography, however (the author), affirms and says that he was of the seed of Shem, the son of Noah. Shem begot Arphaxar, Arphaxar begot Cainan, and Cainan begot Shâlâh and Mâlâh. Shâlâh was written down in the genealogies; but Mâlâh was not, because his affairs were not sufficiently important to be written down in the genealogies. The Book of Adam (iii. 16) says that Cainan was the father of Melchisedek, and that the Angel of the Face, or Michael, appeared to him, and told him that he was going to send away his son from him. This same angel also appeared to Melchisedek and told him to go with Shem, and to minister before the body of Adam in the centre of the earth, and also to Shem. After his interview with the angel, Shem made a splendid coffin to hold the body of Adam, and prepared bread and wine for the journey. When he and Melchisedek went to the Ark to take out the body, they found that the door of it had been locked by Noah, and they had no key to open it. As soon as Melchisedek touched the lock the door opened of itself, and the voice of Adam was heard to address him as the "priest of the Most High God." Melchisedek went into the Ark, and Michael helped him to carry out Adam's body, and Shem brought out the gold, frankincense and myrrh. Shem laid the body in the coffin which he had made, and then shut the door of the Ark. Melchisedek was fifteen years of age when he set out with Shem. The voice of Adam told Shem when they arrived at the centre of the earth, and as soon as the coffin touched the rock, the rock split asunder to receive it. On the following morning Melchisedek builded an altar of twelve stones, and offered up upon it the bread and wine which Shem had brought from Paradise.

Shem's commands to Melchisedek

And Shem said unto Melchisedek, "Thou shalt be the priest of the Most High God, because thou alone hath God chosen to minister before Him in this place. And thou shalt sit (i.e. dwell) here continually, and shalt not depart from this place all the days of thy life. Thou shalt not take a wife, thou shalt not shave thy head, and thou shalt not pour out blood [Fol. 21b, col. 1] in this place. Thou shalt not offer up wild beasts nor feathered fowl, but thou shalt offer up bread and wine always; and thou shalt not build a building in this place. And behold, the Angel of the Lord shall come down to thee and visit thee continually." And Shem embraced and kissed Melchisedek, and blessed him, and he returned to his brethren. And Mâlâkh, the father of Melchisedek, and Yôzâdhâk, his mother, said [unto Shem], "Where is the young man?" And he said, "He died on the journey, and I buried him there" (i.e. where he died); and they mourned for him greatly.

NOTES.--A scribe's note says that in the manuscript of one Makbal Melchisedek's father was called "Harklêîm" and his mother "Shêlâthîêl " (Budge, Book of the Bee, page 34). Melchisedek wore a tunic of skin and a leather girdle, and an angel dwelt with him, and protected him, and gave him food (Book of Adam, iii. 21). When he was old, the kings of the earth heard his fame, and eleven of them gathered together and came to see him; and they entreated him to go with them, but he would not be persuaded. And when he did not conform to their wishes, they built a city for him there, and he called it Jerusalem; and the kings said to one another, "This is the king of all the earth, and the father of nations."

The Generations of Shem

And when Shem had lived six hundred years he died, and Arphakhshar, his son, and Shâlâh (Salah), and `Abhâr (Eber), his sons, buried him.

And Arphakhshar was thirty and five years old when he begot Shâlâh, and all the days of his life were four hundred and thirty-eight years [Fol. 21b, col. 2], and he died, and Shâlâh, his son, and `Abhâr and Pâlâg (Peleg) buried him in Arpakhsharath, the city which he built after his own name.

NOTE.--After Shem the Book of Adam (iii. 22) inserts the name of Cainan, the father of Melchisedek (sic), who lived 589 years. Shem's years are given as 550.

Salah was thirty years old when he begot Eber, and all the days of his life were four hundred and thirty-three years [Ethiopic variant, 408 years], and he died, and Eber, his son, and Peleg, and Ar`ô (Reu) puried hill in Shelîhôn, the city which he built after his own name.

Eber was thirty and four years old when he begot Peleg; and all the days of his life were four hundred and sixty-four [Ethiopic variant, 434] years; and he died, and Peleg his son and Reu and Sorôgh (Serug) buried him in `Ebhrîn, the city which he built after his own name.

Peleg was thirty years old when he begot Reu; and all the days of his life were two hundred and thirty-nine years, and he died [and they buried him in the city of Peleg, which he had built after his own name].

The Migration to the land of Sêntar

And in the days of Peleg all the tribes and families of the children of Noah gathered together, and went up from the East. And they found a [Fol. 22a, col. 1] plain in the land of Sên`ar (Shinar ?), and they all sat down there; and from Adam until this time they were all of one speech and one language. They all spake this language, that is to say, SÛRYÂYÂ (Syrian), which is ÂRÂMÂYÂ (Aramean), and this language is the king of all languages. Now, ancient writers have erred in that they said that Hebrew was the first [language], and in this matter they have mingled an ignorant mistake with their writing. For all the languages there are in the world are derived from Syrian, and all the languages in books are mingled with it. In the writing of the Syrians the left hand stretcheth out to the right hand, and all the children of the left hand (i.e. the heathen) draw nigh to the right hand of God; now with the Greeks, and Romans, and the Hebrews, the right hand stretcheth out to the left. [Both Hebrew and Syriac are written from right to left, but Greek and Latin from left to right.

And in the days of Peleg the Tower which is in Babel was built, and there the tongues of men were confounded. [A marginal note says, "the division of tongues took place at midnight."] And from that place they were scattered over the face of all the earth; and that place was called "Babel," because tongues were confounded there.

NOTE.--The name Babel or Babylon has nothing to do with the Hebrew words "to mix, to confound." "Babel" is a transcription of the Assyrian words "Bâb-ilu," which mean "Gate of God," and which are the Semitic translation of the Sumerian words KA-DINGIRRA-KI.

And after the division of tongues Peleg died in great sorrow, and with tears in his eyes and grief in his heart, because in his days the earth was divided. And his son Reu, and Serug, and Nâhôr buried him in Peleghîn, the city which he had built after his own name. And there were seventy-two tongues in the earth, and seventy-two heads of tribes (or families), and each tribe and tongue made unto themselves a chief like a king.

The Posterity of Japhet

And the seed of Japhet became thirty-seven nations and kingdoms; viz. Gâmâr (Gomer), and Yâwân, and Mâdhâi, and Tûbîl, and Mâshêkh [Fol. 22b, col. 1], and Tîrês, and all the kingdoms of the Alânâyê; all these are the children of Japhet.

NOTES.--Another list gives: Gomer (Goths), Magog (Galatians), Madai (Medes), Javan (Greeks), Tûbîl (Bithynians), Meshech (Mysians), Tîras (Thracians), and the Anshklâyê. From Gomer sprang the Ashkenaz (Armenians), Danphar (Cappadocians), Togarmah (Asians), and the Isaurians. From Javan sprang Halles (Hellas), Tarshish, Cilicia, Cyprus, Kittim, Doranim (see Gen. x. 4), and the Macedonians. Book of the Bee (chapter xxii).

And the sons of Hâm--Kûsh (Nubia), and Mesrîm (Egypt), and Pôt, and Canaan, and all their children. And the sons of Shem--ʿÎlâm (Elamites), and Âshôr (Assyrians), and Arpakhshar (Persians ?), and Lôdh (Lud), and Ârâm (Arameans, Damascenes, and Harranites), and all their children. Now the children of Japhet clung to the borders of the east, from the Mountain of Nôdh, which is on the confines of the east, to the Tigris and the confines of the north, and from Baktôrônôs (Bactria ?) as far as Gadhrîôn (Gadarea ?).

And the children of Shem held from Persia [in] the east as far as the sea of Tadhrasnkôs in the west; unto them belongeth the middle of the earth, and they held sovereignty and dominion therein. The children of Shem occupy all the southern and a little of the western quarter.

And Reu lived thirty-two years, and begot Serug. And in the days of Reu, in his one hundred [Fol. 22b, col. 2] and thirtieth year, Nimrod, the mighty man, the first king on the earth, reigned, and he reigned sixty-nine years; and the beginning of his kingdom was Babel. This Nimrod saw the figure of a crown in the heavens, and he called Sîsân, the weaver, who wore a crown like unto it, and he set it on his head. And because of this men used to say that the crown came down to him from heaven.

NOTE.--Nimrod became so wicked that he thought he was God. Book of Adam (iii. 23).

THE FOURTH THOUSAND YEARS--FROM THE REIGN OF REU TO THE TWENTY-SIXTH YEAR OF THE LIFE OF EHUD

AND in the days of Reu the Mesrâyê, who are the Egyptians, appointed their first king; his name was Puntos, and he reigned over them sixty-eight years. And in the days of Reu a king reigned in Shebhâ (Sâba), and in Ophir, and in Havilah. And there reigned in Sâba sixty of the daughters of Sâba. And for many years women reigned in Sâba--until the kingdom of Solomon, the son of David. And the children of Ophir, that is, Send (Scindia ?), appointed to be their [Fol. 23a, col. 1] Lophoron (?), who built Ophir with stones of gold; now, all the stones that are in Ophir are of gold. And the children of Havilah appointed to be their king Havîl, who built Havilah, that is, Hend (India ?).

NOTES.--According to the Book of Adam (iii. 23), the first king of Egypt was called Yanuf; he built Memphis, that is, Misr. Sasen reigned in Sâba and built the city of Sâba, the people of which are called "Sabeans." Bahlul, builder of Bahlu, reigned over Lebensa in India. The first king of Sâba is said to have been Menyelek I, the son of Solomon king of Mael and Mâkeda, Queen of Sheba.

And Reu died, being two hundred and thirty-nine years old, and Serug his son, and Nâhôr and Tarah (Terah) buried him in Aor`în, the city which he built after his own name.

And Serug lived thirty years and begot Nâhôr, and all the days of his life were two hundred and thirty years. And in the days of Serug the worship of idols entered the world. And in his days the children of men began to make themselves graven images, and it was at this time that the introduction of idols into the world took place. For the children of men were scattered all over the earth, and they had neither teachers nor lawgivers, and no one to show them [Fol. 23a, col. 2] the way of truth wherein they should walk, and for this reason they became confused and fell into error. Some of them through their error adored the heavens, and some of them worshipped the sun, and moon and stars, and some of them the earth, and wild beasts, and birds, and creeping things, and trees, and stones, and the creatures of the sea, and the waters, and the winds. Now Satan had blinded their eyes so that they might walk in the darkness of error, because they had no hope of a resurrection. For when one of them died they used to make an image of him, and set it up upon his grave, so that the remembrance [of his appearance] might not pass from before their eyes. And error having been sown broadcast in all the earth, the land became filled with idols in the form of men and women. And then Serug died, being two hundred and thirty years old, and Nâhôr, and Tarah [Fol. 23b, col. 1], and Abraham his sons, buried him in Sarghîn, the city which he built after his own name.

And Nâhôr was twenty-nine years old when he begot Terah. And in the days of Nâhôr, in the seventieth year of his life, when God looked upon the children of men, and saw that they were worshipping idols, a great earthquake took place, and all their houses were overturned and fell down; but the people did not understand within themselves, and they added to their wickedness. And Nâhôr died when he was one hundred and forty-seven years old, and Terah his son and Abraham buried him. Terah was seventy-five years old when he begot Abraham.

NOTES.--Nâhôr was the son of Serug by his wife Melka, and he married Iyosaka, the daughter of Kheber, the Chaldean, and she became the mother of Terah. The "Wind Flood" came upon the earth in the days of Nâhôr. God opened the storehouse of the winds and whirlwinds, and they uprooted the idols and graven images, and they collected them together, and buried them under the earth, and they reared over them these mounds that are in the world. (Book of the Bee, chapter xxiii.) God sent forth winds, and the whirlwind, and earthquakes on the earth, until the idols were broken one against another. Instead of repenting, men added to their sins. Book of Adam (iii. 24.)

And Terah was seventy-five years old when he begat Abraham. And in the days of Terah, in his ninetieth year, sorcery appeared on the earth in the city of Aôr (Ur), which Horon, the son of `Abhâr, built. Now, there was in the city a certain man who was very rich, and he died at that time. And his son made an image of him in gold [Fol. 23b, col. 2], and set it up upon his grave, and he appointed there a young man to keep guard over it. And Satan went and took up his abode in that image, and he spake to that youth (i.e. the son of the rich man) after the manner of his father. And thieves went into [his house], and took everything that the youth possessed, and he went out to the tomb of his father weeping. And Satan spake unto him, saying, "Weep not in my presence, but go and fetch thy little son, and slay him here as a sacrifice to me, and forthwith everything which thou hast lost shall be returned to me here." And straightway the youth did as Satan told him, and he slew his son, and bathed in his blood. And Satan went forth immediately from that image [of gold], and entered into the youth, and taught him sorcery, and enchantments, and divination, and the lore of the Chaldeans, and [how to tell] fortunes, and [how to forecast] events, and [how to foretell] destinies. And behold, from that time the children of men began to sacrifice their sons to devils and to worship idols, for the devils entered into the images, and took up their abodes therein.

NOTES.--According to the Book of Adam (iii. 24), the young man who ministered to the image had to sweep the ground around it, and to pour out water before it, and to burn incense. The image seems to have resembled somewhat the Ka-figure of the Egyptians, and its attendant may be regarded as the equivalent of the Ka-priest. A marginal note in the Syriac MS. of the "Cave of Treasures" in the British Museum says that the city Aôr is Erech (Warka). The "Interpreter" (i.e. Theodore), says it was Bêth Mâhôzê (Ctesiphon and Seleucia), that is, Bêth Arâmâyê, but both statements are incorrect. The city referred to is Ur, where, in recent years, excavations have been carried out by the British Museum and the University of Pennsylvania. (See my Babylonian Life and History, London, 1925, and the account of the excavations given at the end of the present work, page 275.)

And in the one hundredth year of the life of Nâhôr, when God saw that the children of men were sacrificing their Sons to devils [Fol. 24a, col. 1], and worshipping idols, He opened the storehouses of the wind, and the gate of the whirlwind, and a blast of wind went forth in all the earth. And it uprooted the images, and the places where offerings were made to devils, and it swept together the idols, and the images, and the pillared buildings in a heap, and piled up great mounds [of earth] over them; [and they are there] to this day. Now to this blast of wind learned men have given the name of "Wind-Flood"; but certain who have erred have said, "These mounds existed [already] in the days of the Flood [of waters]. Now those who have said these things have erred greatly from the truth; for before the Flood [of waters] there were no idols in the earth, and it was not because of idols that the Flood came, but because of the fornication of the daughters of Cain. And, moreover, at that time there were no men on this earth, which was a waste and a desert. And our fathers were cast forth in days of old, as it were, into exile, because they were not worthy to be [Fol. 24a, col. 2] neighbours of Paradise. And through the Ark they were driven forth to the mountains of Kardô, and from there they were scattered about throughout all the earth. For these mounds came into being because of idols, and in them are buried all the idols of that time, and all the devils also who dwell in them are in these mounds, and there is no mound which hath not devils in it.

Nimrod the fire-worshipper, and Yôntôn, son of Noah

And in the days of Nimrod, the mighty man (or giant), a fire appeared which ascended from the earth, and Nimrod went down, and looked at it, and worshipped it, and he established priests to minister there, and to cast incense into it. From that day the Persians began to worship fire, [and they do so] to this day.

And Sîsân, the king, found a spring of water in Drôghîn, and he made a white horse and set it over it, and those who bathed in the water used to worship the horse [Fol. 24b, col. 1]. And from that time the Persians began to worship that (sic) horse. [According to the Book of Adam (iii. 25), the horse was made of gold.]

And Nimrod went to Yôkdôrâ of Nôdh, and when he arrived at the Lake (or Sea) of Atrâs, he found there Yôntôn, the son of Noah. [A marginal note in the Syriac MS. adds, "Noah begot this Yôntôn after the Flood, and he honoured him in many things, and sent him to the east to dwell there."] And Nimrod went down and bathed in the Lake, and he came to Yôntôn and did homage unto him. And Yôntôn said, "Thou art a king; doest thou homage unto me?" And Nimrod said unto him, "It is because of thee that I have come down here"; and he remained with him for three years. And Yôntôn taught Nimrod wisdom, and the art of revelation (divining ?), and he said unto him, "Come not back again to me."

And when Nimrod went up from the east, and began to practise the art of divining, very many men marvelled at him. And when Îdhâshîr (Ardeshir ?), the priest who ministered to the fire that ascended from the earth, saw that Nimrod was practising these exalted courses, he entreated the devil, who appeared in connection with that fire, to teach him [Fol. 24b, col. 2] the wisdom of Nimrod. And as the devils were in the habit of destroying those who came nigh unto them by sin, the devil said unto the priest, "A man cannot become a priest and a Magian until he hath known carnally his mother, and his daughter, and his sister." And Îdhâshîr the priest did this, and from that time the priests, and the Magians, and the Persians take their mothers, and their sisters, and their daughters [to wife]. And this Îdhâshîr, the Magian, was the first to begin to study the Signs of the Zodiac, and [omens concerning] luck, and fate, and happenings, and motions of the eyes and eyelids, as well as all the other arts of the learning of the Chaldees. Now, all this learning is the error of devils, and those who practise it shall receive, together with the devils, the doom of the Judgment. And because this art of divination, which was employed by Nimrod, was taught to him [Fol. 25a, col. 1] by Yôntôn, none of the orthodox doctors have suppressed it; nay, they have even practised it. Now the Persians call it "Gelyânâ" (i.e. "Revelation") and the Romans "Estrômîôn" (i.e. "Astronomy"). But that [knowledge] which the Magians have, viz. astrology, is sorcery and the teaching of devils. There are some who say that it doth indeed [teach concerning] luck, and happenings (i.e. future events), and fate, but these are in error. Now Nimrod builded strong cities in the east, Babel, and Nineveh, and Râsân (Râs `Ain), and Selîk: (Seleucia), and Ctesiphon, and Âdhôrbaighân; and he made three fortresses.

The History of Abraham

And Terah, the father of Abraham, lived two hundred and fifty years, and he died, and Abraham and Lot buried him in Hârrân. And there God spoke unto Abraham, and said unto him, "Get thee forth from thy land, and from among thy people, and come to the land which I will show thee." And Abraham took his household, Sârâ his wife [Fol. 25a, col. 2], and Lot, his brother's son, and he went up to the land of the Amôrâyê (Amorites); and he was seventy-five years old when he crossed the desert from the Euphrates. And he was eighty years old when he pursued the kings, and rescued Lot, his brother's son.

NOTES.--When still a boy, Abraham had no belief in idols, and, according to the Kebra Nagast (chapter xiii), "when he was twelve years old his father sent him to sell idols. And Abraham said, 'These are not gods that can make deliverance'; and he took away the idols to sell even as his father had commanded him. And he said unto those unto whom he would sell them, 'Do ye wish to buy goods that cannot make deliverance, things made of wood, and stone, and iron, and brass, which the hand of an artificer hath made?' And they (the people) refused to buy the idols from Abraham because he himself had defamed the images of his father. [An old tradition says that Terah made idols of mud, and it is possible that some of these may be represented by the terra-cotta figures of gods and goddesses which have been found in such large numbers in recent years at Ur and other ancient sites in Babylonia.] And as he was returning he stepped aside from the road, and he set the images down, and looked at them, and said unto them, 'I wonder now if ye are able to do what I ask you at this moment, and whether ye are able to give me bread to eat or water to drink?' And none of them answered him, for they were pieces of stone and wood; and he abused them and heaped revilings upon them, and they spake never a word. And he buffeted the face of one, and kicked another with his feet, and a third he knocked over and broke to pieces with stones, and he said unto them, 'If ye are unable to save yourselves from him that buffeteth you, and ye cannot requite with injury him that injureth you, how can ye be called "gods"? Those who worship you do so in vain, and as for myself I utterly despise you, and ye shall not be my gods.' Then he turned his face to the East, and he stretched out his hands and said, 'Be Thou my God, O Lord, Creator of the heavens and the earth, Creator of the Sun and Moon, Creator of the sea and the dry land, Maker of the majesty of the heavens and the earth, and of that which is visible and that which is invisible; O Maker of the universe, be Thou my God. I place my trust in Thee, and from this day forth I will place my trust in no other save Thyself.' And then there appeared unto him a chariot of fire which blazed, and Abraham was afraid, and fell on his face on the ground; and God said unto him, 'Fear thou not, stand upright.'"

On the day of the birth of Abraham the house shone with a bright light. Many people fell down, and there was a cry in a loud voice, which said, "Woe is me! Woe is me! For he who shall crush my kingdom hath been born." And he who cried out wept, and described the events which should take place, saying, "It is he who shall burn down my abode." And there were among the people certain men who said, "Kill this child forthwith," and those who spake thus knew well that grace would be given to Abraham. And God set mercy in the heart of the father of Abraham, and he said to the Satans, "Whence come ye, O ye who tell me that I should kill my son who is a gracious gift of God?" And he reared the child . . . . . And Abraham was circumcised by the hand of Gabriel and Michael, who helped him. From the Book of the Mysteries of Heaven and Earth, ed. Perruchon.

Abraham and Melchisedek

And at that time Abraham had no son, because Sârâ was barren.

And when he returned from the battle of the kings, the agency of God called him, and he crossed the mountain of Yâbhôs (Jebus ?), and Melchisedek, the king of Shâlîm, the priest of the Most High God, went forth to meet him. And when Abraham saw Melchisedek, he made haste and fell upon his face, and did homage to him, and he rose up from the ground and embraced him, and kissed him, and was blessed by him; and Melchisedek blessed Abraham. And Abraham gave Melchisedek tithes of everything which he had with him, and Melchisedek made him to participate in the Holy Mysteries, [of] the bread of the Offering and the wine of redemption. And after [Fol. 25b, col. 1] Melchisedek had blessed him, and made him to participate in the Holy Mysteries, God spake unto Abraham, and said unto him, "Thy reward is exceedingly great. Since Melchisedek hath blessed thee, and hath made thee to partake of bread and wine [with him], I also will assuredly bless thee, and I will assuredly multiply thy seed."

And when Abraham was eighty-six years old Ishmael was born to him by Hâghâr, the Egyptian woman, whom Pharaoh had given to Sârâ as a handmaiden. Now Sârâ was the sister of Abraham on the father's side, because Terah took two women to wife. When Yâwnû, the mother of Abraham, died, Terah took to wife a woman whose name was "Naharyath" (or Shalmath, or Tona, or Tahdif), and of her Sârâ was born. It was because of this [fact] that Abraham said, "She is my sister, the daughter of my father, but not the daughter of my mother" (Gen. xx. 2, 5).

The Birth of Isaac

And Abraham was ninety-nine [Fol. 25b, col. 2] years old when God went into his house and gave Sârâ a son, and he was one hundred years old when Isaac was born to him. And Isaac was thirteen years old when his father took him and went up to the mountain of Yâbhôs (Jebus) to Melchisedek, the priest of God, the Most High. Now Mount Yâbhôs is the mountain of the Amôrâyê (Amorites), and in that place the Cross of Christ was set up, and on it grew the tree which held the ram that saved Isaac. And that same place is the centre of the earth, and the grave of Adam, and the altar of Melchisedek, and Golgotha, and Karkaftâ, and Gefîftâ (Gabbatha). And there David saw the angel bearing the sword of fire. There, too, Abraham took up Isaac his son for a burnt offering, and he saw the Cross, and Christ [Fol. 26a, col. 1], and the redemption of our father Adam. The tree (i.e. thicket) was a symbol of the Cross of Christ our Lord, and the ram [caught] in its branches was the mystery of the manhood of the Word, the Only One. And, because of this, Paul cried out and said, "If they had only known [it] they were not crucifying the Lord of glory." Let the mouths of the heretics be stopped who in their madness impute passibility to the Eternal God.

Now, when Christ was eight days old, Joseph, the betrothed of Mary, rose up to circumcise the Child according to the Law, and he circumcised Him according to the custom that was the Law. In like manner Abraham took up his son as an offering, but he at the same time [fore]saw in this [act] the crucifixion of Christ. And this thing did Christ openly proclaim before the multitudes of the Jews, saying, "Abraham, your father, wanted to see My days, and he saw and was glad" (John viii. 56). Abraham saw the day of the redemption [Fol. 26a, col. 2] of Adam, and he saw and rejoiced, and it was revealed unto him that Christ would suffer on behalf of Adam.

The founding of Jerusalem

And in that same year in which Abraham offered up his son as an offering, in that same year [I say] Jerusalem was built; and the beginning of the building thereof was in this wise. Melchisedek having appeared and shown himself to men, the kings of the nations heard his history, and they gathered together and came unto him.

The names of the kings who built Jerusalem

Abimelech, king of Gâdhâr.
Âmarphîl, (Amraphel), king of Sen`âr.
Arioch, king of Dâlâsâr (sic).
Kardla`mar (Chedorlaomer), king of Elam.
Tar`îl (Tidal), king of the Gîlâyê.
Bârâ (Bera), king of Sodom.
Barshâ (Birsha), king of Gomorrah.
Shênâbh (Shinab), king of Adhâmâh.
Shamâ`ir (Shemeber), king of Zeboim.
Salâkh, king of Bâlâ`.

Tâbhîk, king of Damascus.

Baktôr, king of the desert.

These twelve kings gathered together and came to Melchisedek, king of Shâlim [Fol. 26b, col. 1], the priest of the Most High God. And when they saw his appearance, and heard his words, they entreated him to go with them. And he said unto them, "I am not able to go from this place to any other"; and they took counsel together about building him a city, and said to each other, "Verily, he is the king of the whole earth, and the father of all kings." And they built him a city and made Melchisedek to live in it; and Melchisedek called the name thereof "Jerusalem." And when Mâghôgh, the king of the south, heard [of this], he came to him, and saw his appearance, and spake unto him, and gave him offerings and gifts. And Melchisedek was held in honour by all, and he was called the "Father of Kings."

Melchisedek

Now, as concerning what the Apostle said, "there was no beginning to his days, and no end to his life" (Heb. vii. 3) [Fol. 26b, col. 2], it has been thought by simple folk that he was not a man at all, and in their error they have said concerning him that he was God. God forbid that there should have been no beginning to his days or end to his life. [The Apostle spake thus] because when Shem, the son of Noah, took away Melchisedek from his parents, no word is said as to how old he was when he went up from the East, and it is not said how old he was at the time of his departure from this world. Now, he was the son of Mâlâkh, the son of Arpakhshar, the son of Shem, and he was not the son of one of the Patriarchs. And the Apostle said that none of his father's family had ever ministered at the altar (Heb. vii. 6). The name of his father is not written in the genealogies, because Matthew and Luke, the Evangelists [only] wrote down the [names of the] Fathers [in chief, i.e. Patriarchs]; and for this reason neither the name of his father [Fol. 27a, col. 1], nor the name of his mother, is known. The Apostle did not say that he had no parents, but [only] that they were not written down in Matthew and Luke.

Kûmrôs

And in the one hundredth year [of the life] of Abraham there was a king in the East whose name was "Kûmrôs." He built Shemesht (Samosata), after the name of his son Shemeshtô, and Klawdîya (Claudias), after the name of his daughter Kâlôdh, and Pîrîn after the name of his son Pôrôn.

Nimrod founds Nisibis, Harrân and Edessa

And in the fiftieth year of [the life of] Reu, Nimrod went up and built Nisibis, and Edessa, and Harrân, which is Edessa. And Harrânîth, the wife of Dâsân, the priest of the mountain, surrounded it with a wall, and the people of Harrân made a statue of her and worshipped her. And Baltîn, who was given to Tamûzâ (Tammuz)--now because B'êlshemîn loved her, Tammuz fled before him--set fire to Harrân and burned it.

The Death of Sârâ

And when Sârâ, the wife of Abraham, died, Abraham took to wife Kentôrâ [Fol. 27a, col. 2], the daughter of Baktôr, the king of the desert. And there were born unto him by her Zamrân, and Yakshân, and Mâdhân, and Medhyân, and Ashbâk, and Shôh. [See Gen. xxv. 1, 2; 1 Chron. i. 32. A marginal note in the Syriac MS. says, "these sons of Kentôrâ are called sons of Daran by the prophet."] And from these are sprung the Arabs.

Isaac and Rebecca

And when Isaac was forty years old, Eliezer, a son of the house of Abraham, went down and brought Rabkâ (Rebecca) from the east, and Isaac took her to wife. And when Abraham died Isaac buried him by the side of Sârâ.

NOTE.--According to the Book of Adam (iv. 4), Abraham was 175 years old when he died, and Isaac and Ishmael buried him. Rebecca was the daughter of Bethuel, the Aramean, a native of the town of Arâch (Erech ?).

And when Isaac was sixty years old Rebecca became with child of Esau and Jacob. And being sorely afflicted, she went to Melchisedek, and he prayed over her and said unto her, "Two nations are in thy womb, and two peoples shall be removed from thy loins, that is to say, shall go forth from thy womb. One nation shall be stronger than the other, and the elder shall be in subjection to the younger, that is to say, Esau [Fol. 27b, col. 1] shall be in subjection to Jacob."

The founding of Jericho

And in the sixty-seventh year of [the life of] Isaac, Jericho was built by seven kings, namely, the king of the Hittites, and the king of the Amorites, and the king of the Girgantes, and the king of the Jebusites, and the king of the Canaanites, and the king of the Hivites, and the king of the Perizites; and each of them surrounded it with a wall. Now the son of Mesrîn (Mizraim), the king of the Egyptians, had founded Jericho in olden time. And Ishmael made a mill of the hands (i.e. a handmill) in the desert, a mill of slavery (i.e. a mill to be worked by, slaves).

Jacob's Ladder

And in the one hundred and third year of his life Isaac blessed Jacob, who was forty years old, and having received the blessing from his father, he went down into the desert [Fol. 27b, col. 2] of Beersheba, and lay down to sleep there; and when he was lying down he took a stone and made a pillow of it. And he saw in his dream, and behold, a ladder was set upon the earth. And the top of it was in the heavens. And the angels of God were going up and coming down, and the Lord stood at the top of it. And Jacob woke up from his sleep, and said, "This is truly the house of God"; and he took the stone of his pillow, and made it an altar, and he anointed it with oil. And he vowed a vow and said, "Of everything which I have will I tithe for this stone." Now, it is manifest to those who possess understanding that the ladder which Jacob saw symbolizeth the Cross of our Redeemer. And the angels who were going up and down were the ministers of Zechariah and Mary, and the Magi, and the shepherds. And the Lord Who was standing at [Fol. 28a, col. 1] the top of the ladder symbolized Christ, Who stood on the Cross that He might go down to redeem us.

NOTES.--The Power of God which was upon the top of the ladder was [a type of] the manifestation of God the Word in pure flesh of the formation of Adam. The place in which it appeared was a type of the Church; the stone under his head, which he set up for an altar, was a type of the altar; and the oil which he poured out upon it was like the holy oil wherewith they anoint the altar. Book of the Bee (chapter xxvii).

Jacob and Baptism

And when God had shown the blessed Jacob the Cross of Christ by means of the Ladder of the Angels, and the coming down of Christ for our redemption, and the Church, the House of God, and the altar by means of the stone, and the offerings by means of the tithes, and the anointing by means of the oil, Jacob again went down to the East that there God might show him baptism. And Jacob looked, and saw, and beheld three flocks of sheep lying down by a well; and there was a great stone placed over the mouth of the well. And Jacob drew nigh, and rolled away the stone from the mouth of the well, and watered the sheep of his mother's brother. And having watered the flocks, he took Rachel and kissed her.

Now by "Well" [Fol. 28a, col. 2] the blessed Jacob indicated (or, depicted) baptism, which was covered over (i.e. hidden) from the races of men, and generations and tribes. And the three flocks of sheep which were lying down by the well are a type of the three divisions and three groups [who come] for baptism, namely, men and women and children. And that Jacob saw Rachel coming with the flocks, and that he neither embraced her nor kissed her until he had rolled away the stone from the well, and she had watered the flocks, is in accordance with the law of the sons of the Church, who neither embrace nor kiss the Lamb of Christ until baptism hath opened [the way]; they go down into the waters and put on strength from them and then the sons of the Church embrace and kiss. And as Jacob served with Laban for seven years, and the woman he loved was not given to him, so also was it with the Jews, who served Pharaoh, king of Egypt, in slavery, and went forth. [Fol. 28b, col. 1.] For the Covenant of the Church, the Bride of Christ, was not given unto them, but that Covenant which was old, and worn out, and of no effect. Now the eyes of [Leah], the first woman whom Jacob took to wife, were hateful, whilst the eyes of Rachel were beautiful, and her countenance was radiant. A covering (i.e. veil) was laid over the face of the first Covenant, so that the children of Israel might not see the beauty thereof; as for the second Covenant, it is wholly light.

Jacob's sons. The Death of Isaac

Jacob was seventy-seven years old when he received the blessing of Isaac, his father, and he was eighty-nine years old when he begot Reuben, his firstborn, by Leah. The sons of Jacob are these:--

Reuben, Simeon, Levi, Judah, Issachar and Zebulon; these are the sons of Leah.
Joseph and Benjamin were the sons of Rachel.

Gad and Asher were the sons of Zilpah, the handmaiden of Leah [Fol. 28b, col. 2].

Dan and Naphtali were the sons of Bilhah, the handmaiden of Rachel.

And after twenty years Jacob returned to Isaac his father. And all the days of the life of Isaac were one hundred and eighty years--until the thirty-first year of the life of Levi--and he died in the one hundred and twentieth year of the life of Jacob. Twenty-three years after Jacob went up from Harrân, Joseph was sold to the Midianites; he was sold during the lifetime of Isaac, and they mourned for him. When Isaac died Jacob and Esau, his sons, buried him with Abraham and Sârâ. Seven years later Rebecca died, and was buried with Abraham, and Isaac, and Sârâ; and Rachel died and was buried with them.

And Judah, the son of Jacob, took unto himself to wife Shû` (Shuah), the Canaanitess [Fol. 29a, col. 1], and his father was grieved because he had taken to wife a woman of the seed of Canaan. And Jacob said unto Judah, "May the Lord God of our fathers Abraham and Isaac not permit the seed of Canaan to be mingled with our families." And there were born unto Judah by Shuah, the Canaanite woman, `Îr (Er), Ônân, and Shêlâ (Shelah). And Judah took a wife for Er his firstborn, Tâmâr, and he consorted with her unnaturally, and God put him to death. And Judah gave Tâmâr to Ônân, and as soon as his seed became available for Tâmâr he wasted it, and him also did God put to death. Thus, God did not permit the seed of Canaan to mingle with the seed of Jacob, even as Jacob prayed God that the seed of Canaan, the firstborn of the lascivious Ham, might not be mingled among the generations [Fol. 29a, col. 2] of the Fathers. And God made Tâmâr go out to the roadside, and Judah lay with her in the passion of fornication, and she conceived and brought forth Peres (Pharez) and Zarah.

Jacob in Egypt

And Jacob and all his descendants went down into Egypt to Joseph, and he lived in Egypt seventeen years; and Jacob died, being one hundred and forty years old, and Joseph was fifty-six years old when his father died, in the twelfth year of Kâhâth. And the wise physicians of Pharaoh embalmed him, and Joseph took him up [to Canaan] and buried him with Abraham and Isaac his father.

NOTE.--According to the Book of Adam (iv. 5), Jacob lived in Egypt fourteen years, and died there at the age of 157 years, when Joseph was 53 years old.

The Genealogies of the "Tribes" and the "Children of Israel"

Now there are certain doctors who trace the genealogies of the Tribes from the death of Jacob, and who mix them together, but they do not do this in the light of knowledge. They set in the midst two genealogies, one of the "Tribes," and the other of the "Children of Israel" [Fol. 29b, col. 1]. Now fix thine attention on these generations, and how they became mixed together. [When] they went forth from Egypt: Judah begot Pharez, Pharez begot Hesrôn (Hezron), Hezron begot Ârâm (Râm, 1 Chron. ii. 9), Ârâm begot Amminadab, Amminadab begot Nahshôn (Nahson), and Nahshôn was he who became prince of Judah. And Amminadab gave the sister of Nahshôn to ʿÎr (so in the text, but read Eleazar), the son of Aaron, the priest; of her was born Phinehas, the great priest, who prayed "and the plague was stayed" (Num. xxv. 7, 8; Ps. cvi. 30). Behold, I have shown thee that from Amminadab, the priesthood of the children of Israel was transmitted by the sister of Nahshôn, and the kingdom by Nahshôn her brother. Observe also that the priesthood and the kingdom were transmitted by Judah to the children of Israel.

And Nahshôn begot Shîlâ, that is to say, Salmôn, and Shîlâ begot Boaz. Observe now that the kingdom went forth from Boaz and Ruth [Fol. 29b, col. 2], the Moabitess, for the old man Boaz took Ruth to wife so that Lot, the son of Abraham's brother, might have participation in the transmission of the kingdom. And God did not deprive the righteous man Lot of the reward of his labour, because he had suffered in exile with Abraham, and he received the angels of God in peace. And that the righteous man Lot might not be reviled because he slept with his daughters, God granted that the royal succession might be maintained by the seed of both, and that Christ should be born of the seed of Lot and Abraham. And from the seed of Ruth, the Moabitess, Obed was born, and from Obed, Jesse, and from Jesse, David, and from David, Solomon; these are the descendants of Ruth, the Moabitess, the daughter of Lot. And of Naʿmâ (Naamah, 1 Kings xiv. 21), the Ammonitess, another daughter of Lot, whom Solomon took to wife [Fol. 30a, col. 1], was born Rehoboam, who reigned after Solomon.

Solomon

Now Solomon married many wives, seven hundred free-born women, and three hundred concubines; and of the thousand women which he took to wife, he had no son except from Naamab the Ammonitess. And why was it that God did not give him a son from these [others]? It was in order to prevent the wicked seed of the Canaanites, and Jebusites, and Amorites, and Hittites, and Gergasites, and the seed of the peoples whom God hated, from mingling in the succession of the genealogy of Jesus Christ.

NOTE from the Kebra Nagast, chapter lxvii.--And the Angel of God went down to Solomon and said unto him, "From being a wise man thou hast turned thyself into a fool, and from being a rich man thou hast turned thyself into a poor man, and from being a king thou hast turned thyself into a man of no account, through transgressing the commandment of God. And the beginning of thy evil was the taking of many wives by thee, for through this thou didst transgress His Law, and His decree, and the ordinance of God which Moses wrote and gave to you, to Israel, that ye should not marry wives from alien peoples, but only from your kinsfolk and the house of your fathers, that your seed might be pure and holy, and that God might dwell with you. But thou didst hold lightly the Law of God, thinking that thou wast wiser than God, and that thou wouldst get very many male children. But the foolishness of God is wiser than the wisdom of men, and he hath only given thee three sons: the one who carried off thy glory into an alien land, and made the habitation of God to be in Ethiopia; the one who is lame of foot, who shall sit upon thy throne for the people of Israel, the son of the kin of thy kin from Tarbâna, of the house of Judah; and the one who is the son of a Greek woman, a handmaiden, who in the last days shall destroy Rehoboam and all thy kin of Israel; and this land shall be his because he believeth in Him that shall come, the Saviour

The chiefs of Israel born in Egypt

Now the succession of the children of Israel is this: Levi, and Amram, and Moses, and Joshua, the son of Nôn, and Caleb, the son of Yôfannâ (Jephunneh). These were born in Egypt.

NOTE.--Moses was the son of Amram, the son of Kohath, the son of Levi; his mother's name was Yokâbâr (Jochebed). Book of the Bee (chapter xxix).

Moses

And when Moses was born he was cast into the river, and Shîpôr (in Ethiopic, Sephurah), the Egyptian woman, the daughter of Pharaoh, took him up, and he lived in the house of Pharaoh for forty years. And then [Fol. 30a, col. 2] he killed Pethkôm, the Egyptian, the chief of the bakers of Pharaoh. Now this was noised abroad in the house of Pharaoh, after Pharaoh's daughter Makrî, who was called "Shîpôr Mesrên (i.e. "Trumpet of Egypt"), was dead, and Moses was afraid, and he fled to Midian, to Reuel, the Cushite, the priest of Midian.

NOTES.--Moses was a beautiful child, and was called "Pantîl" (Paltîêl ?), and "Amlâkyâ," and the Egyptians used to call him the "Shakwîthâ of Pharaoh's daughter." Various names are given to this princess, e.g. Makrî, Mary, Shîpôr, Tharmesîs, Tarmûthîsâ; Bar Hebraeus says she was the daughter of Amûnpthîs, or Amûnpâthîôs. Book of the Bee (chapter xxix).

And Moses took to wife Zipporah, the Cushite woman, daughter of the priest, and two sons were born to him--Gershom and Eliezer. And in the second year of the life of Moses, Joshua, the son of Nôn, was born in Egypt. And Moses was eighty years old when God talked with him from out of the bush, and because of his fear his tongue halted, even as he said to God, "Behold, my Lord, from the day wherein Thou didst speak to me I have been halting of tongue." Moses lived in Egypt forty years, and in the house [Fol. 30b, col. 1] of the priest of Midian forty years, and he passed forty years in governing the people. And he died at the age of one hundred and twenty years on Mount Nebo.

NOTES.--From Adam until the death of Moses was 3,868 years. Book of the Bee (chapter xxx). MOSES' ROD.-Adam cut the rod from a branch of the Tree of Good and Evil which grew in Paradise, and he used it as a staff all his life. It passed from hand to hand to Abraham, who smashed his father's idols with it. It went with him to Egypt, and when it came to Jacob he used it as a shepherd's crook. Judah received it and gave it to Tamar, and then an angel laid it up in the Cave of Treasures until Midian was built. An angel showed Jethro the Cave, and he took the rod from it, and from him it went of its own free will to Moses. The rod became a serpent, and it swallowed up the rod of Pôsdî, the sorceress. The rod was taken unto the promised land by Joshua, and Phineas hid it in the dust at the gate of Jerusalem, where it remained until Christ showed it to Joseph, who took it to Egypt and brought it back to Nazareth. It passed to James, the brother of our

Lord, but was stolen by Judas Iscariot, who gave it to the Jews who were crucifying our Lord; to them it "became a judgment and a fall." Book of the Bee (chapter xxx).

The Successors of Moses

And Joshua, the son of Nôn, was the governor of the children of Israel for twenty-seven years. And after the death of Joshua, the son of Nôn, Kûshân, the Wicked (Chushanrishathayim), was lord over the people for eighty years.

And ˋAthnâîl (Othniel), the son of Kenaz, the brother of Caleb, the son of Jephunneh, was lord over Israel for forty years.

And then the children of Israel were in subjection to the Moabites for eighteen years.

And Ahôr (Ehud), the son of Gera, ruled the children of Israel for eighty years.

THE FIFTH THOUSAND YEARS. FROM THE TWENTY-SIXTH YEAR OF EHUD'S LIFE TO THE SECOND YEAR OF THE REIGN OF CYRUS

Nâbhîn (Jabin), who was dried up in body, ruled twenty years.

DEBORAH and Barak [ruled them] forty years. The children [Fol. 30b, col. 2] of Israel were in subjection to the Midianites seven years, and God delivered them by the hands of Gideon, who ruled them forty years.

Abimelech his son reigned after him three years.

Tûla' (Tola), the son of Puah [ruled them] twenty-three years.

Yâîr, the Gileadite, twenty-two years.

And again the children of Israel were in subjection to the Ammonites eighteen years, and God delivered them by the hand of Naphtah (Jephthah), the man who offered up his daughter as a sacrifice, and he ruled them six years.

Abhîsân (Ibzan of Bethlehem), who is Nahshôn (sic), ruled them seven years.

Alôn (Elon), who was from Zebulon, ruled them ten years.

`Abhrôn (Abdon, the son of Hillel, the Pirathonite) ruled them eight years.

And the children of Israel were in subjection to the Philistines forty years, and God delivered them by the hand of Samson, and he ruled them twenty years.

And the [Fol. 31a, col. 1] children of Israel lived without a governor for eighteen years, and then Eli the priest rose up and ruled them forty years.

And Samuel rose up over them and ruled them twenty years. And in the days of Samuel the children of Israel provoked to wrath God, Who had delivered them from the servitude of the Egyptians, and they made Saul, the son of Kish, king, and he reigned over them forty years.

And in the days of Saul lived Gûlyâdh (Goliath), a giant of the Philistines. He came nigh and reviled Israel, and blasphemed against God, and David, the son of Jesse, killed him. And David was praised in songs by the daughters of Israel, and Saul persecuted him. And the Philistines slew Saul because he forsook the Lord, and took refuge with the devils.

NOTE.--The story of David and Goliath finds an interesting parallel in the history of Sanehat as found in an Egyptian papyrus in the Royal Library at Berlin. Sanehat fled from Egypt as the result of some political trouble, and made his way into Palestine, where he settled down and prospered, and became a shêkh of great influence and importance. Then a certain man of Thennu went to Sanehat's tent and reviled him, and challenged him to fight him. This man was a mighty warrior, and was famed throughout the country for his strength, and valour, and success. During the following night Sanehat made ready his dagger, and spear, and bow, and at daybreak all the tribes came to the place to witness the great duel which was to take place. The man of Thennu grasped his shield and his battle-axe, and then began to hurl his spears at Sanehat, but they either went wide or Sanehat managed in some way to avoid them; in any case, they failed to touch him. When the man of Thennu saw this, he lost his temper, and made a rush at Sanehat, meaning to close with him and despatch him with his battle-axe. But as he came on in his mad rage Sanehat hurled his short javelin at his head, and it pierced his neck and remained fast in it. The man of Thennu uttered a prolonged shriek and then fell headlong on the ground, face downwards. Sanehat went to him, and, taking his foe's weapons from him, killed him with them. Then he took his stand on the dead body, and shouted the cry of victory, and the onlookers rejoiced in his triumph and applauded him.

David reigned over [Fol. 31a, col. 2] the children of Israel forty years, and Solomon, his son, reigned forty years.

And Solomon did great and wonderful things, and it was he who sent to Ophir and brought gold from the mountains of gold, and the ships sailed the sea for thirty-six months, and then came forth (i.e. returned). It was he who built Tadmor (Palmyra) in the wilderness, and he carried out there great and wonderful works. And when Solomon passed the borders of the mountain which is called Sâ`êr, he found there the altar which Pîôrzâkhâr, and Pîôrzânâi, and Neznâdhôr had built. These were they whom Nimrod, the giant, sent to Balaam, the priest of the Mountain of Sâ`êr, because he heard that he was wont to consult the Signs of the Zodiac, and when they were passing the skirts of the mountain they built there an altar to the sun. And when Solomon saw it he built a city there and called its name "Nîâpôlîs " (more correctly, Heliopolis) [Fol. 31b, col. 1], that is to say, "City of the Sun." And Solomon also built Aradus (Arvad) in the midst of the sea, and he became so famous and renowned that the report of his wise acts went out into all the ends of the earth. And the Queen of Sheba went to hold converse with him. And Solomon loved Hiram, king of Tyre, greatly. And Hiram reigned in Tyre five hundred years, from the days of the kingdom of David to the [days of] the kingdom of Zedekiah and of all the kings of the children of Israel. And at length he forgot that he was a man, and he blasphemed and said, "I am God, and I sit upon the throne of God in the middle of the sea." And Nebuchadnezzar the king killed him.

NOTE.--Solomon reigned over his large kingdom with the greatest wisdom ever found. But he did not keep his soul; but inclined his heart to the love of women, and forsook God, Who had created him and given him his kingdom. And he died in his denial of Him, and in his sins. Book of Adam (iv. 8.)

The purple linen of Tyre

And in the days of Hiram the purple-[coloured] apparel worn by kings [first] appeared. As a dog was running along the sea-shore [at Tyre] he saw a purple shell-fish (i.e. the murex) coming up out of the [Fol. 31b, col. 2] water, and he bit it, and straightway his mouth was filled with the blood of that shell-fish. And a certain shepherd who saw the dog brought a piece of woollen cloth and wiped the dog's mouth with it. And he made that piece of woollen cloth into a crown (i.e. a kafîyah or head-cloth), and set it upon his head, and as he walked along in the sun, those who saw him thought that rays of fire were coming forth from his head, and when Hiram heard [of this] he sent for the man. And when he saw the woollen cloth he marvelled, and was astonished. And all the dyers gathered together and marvelled at it, and they set out to enquire into the matter; and they found some of these shell-fish and rejoiced greatly.

The Apostasy of Solomon

And Solomon waxed exceedingly great. And the food [provided for his table every day] consisted of forty oxen, one hundred head of sheep, thirty measures of fine flour, sixty measures of wheat, and three hundred measures of wine; and besides all this [Fol. 32a, col. 1], stags, and gazelle, and wild antelopes, and other creatures of the desert. And he became froward and transgressed the Law, and hearkened not to the commands of his father, and he took to wife one thousand women from all the peoples whom God hated. And in the time of his old age he gave himself up to women, and he let them play with him, and he hearkened to their words, and did their will. And he denied the God of David, his father. And he builded altars to devils, and offered up sacrifices to idols and graven images, and he worshipped the work of the hands; and God turned away His face from him and he died. And he reigned in Jerusalem forty-six years.

NOTE.--Solomon was seduced into idolatry by his wife, the daughter of Pharaoh. "One day she beautified and scented herself for him, and she behaved herself haughtily towards him, and treated him disdainfully. And he said unto her, 'What shall I do? Thou hast made thy face evil towards me, and thy regard towards me is not as it was formerly, and thy beautiful form is not as enticing as usual. Ask me, and I will give thee whatsoever thou wishest, and I will perform it for thee, so that thou mayest make thy face gracious towards me as formerly'; but she held her peace and answered him never a word. And he repeated to her the words that he would do whatsoever she wished. And she said unto him, 'Swear to me by the God of Israel that thou wilt not play me false.' And he swore to her that he would give her whatsoever she asked for, and that he would do for her everything she told him. And she tied a scarlet thread on the middle of the door of [the house of] her gods, and she brought three locusts and set them in the house of her gods. And she said unto Solomon, 'Come to me without breaking the scarlet thread, bend thyself and kill these locusts before me, and pull out their necks,' and he did so. And she said unto him, 'I will henceforward do thy will, for thou hast sacrificed to my gods and hast worshipped them.' Now he had done this because of his oath, so that he might not break his oath which she had made him to swear, even though he knew that it was an offence (or, sin) to enter into the house of her gods." Kebra Nagast (chapter lxiv).

Rehoboam

And Rehoboam, the son of Solomon, reigned after him. Rehoboam was forty-one years old when [he began] to reign, and he polluted Jerusalem with fornication, and the altars of devils, and the stink of heathendom; and the kingdom of Israel was rent in twain. And in the fifth year [Fol. 32a, col. 2] of his kingdom Shishak, the king of Egypt, went up against Jerusalem. And he carried off all the treasure of the service of the house of the Lord, and all the treasure of the kingdom of David, and of that of Solomon, and the vessels of gold and the vessels of silver. And he magnified himself and said, "I am not taking away treasure which is yours but the wealth which your fathers tok out of Egypt." And Rehoboam died in the heathen practices of his father Solomon.

Shishak was the first king of the XXIInd Dynasty and reigned about 20 years (947-928 B.C.): he was of Libyan origin. The Egyptian form of his name is SHASHANQ   𓎛𓎛 , and it is found with his title "beloved of Amen" in a cartouche thus:

And Abijah his son reigned after him and he destroyed Jerusalem with fornication and with heathen works--now, Melkâ, the mother of `Abhd-Shâlôm, was his mother--and he died in the heathen practices of his father.

And Asa his son reigned after him for forty years in Jerusalem. He did that which was good before the Lord, and he put away fornication from Jerusalem, and made an end of the heathen practices of his people, for he kept the commandments of God [Fol. 32b, col. 1]. And he drove them (i.e. the idolators) out of his palace (or, kingdom), and made them to be a mockery before all the people, because they [taught] the offering of sacrifices to idols. And Zerah of Judah went up against him, and God humbled him before Asa. And Asa died in righteousness like his father David.

NOTE.--The Book of Adam (iv. 8) says that Asaph (i.e. Asa) took his mother Anna, who was an adulteress, and cast her down from the roof of her house, and she died. Zerah, who is called Eleazar, is described as a "black king" who reigned at Endena. No mention of Zerah the Cushite has hitherto been found in the cuneiform or hieroglyphic inscriptions.

And Jehosaphat his son reigned after him, and he walked in the ways of Asa his father, and he did that which was pleasing before God. And God was angry with him because he was a friend of the house of Ahab, and for this reason God did not permit him to bring out gold from Ophir. Now he made ships to send thither, and they were broken at Ezion Geber. He was thirty-two years old when he began to reign, and the name of his mother was `Azôbhâ (Azuba ?), the daughter of Shâlâh. And Jehosaphat died in his righteousness.

Joram reigned after him, and he was thirty-two years old [Fol. 32b, col. 2] when he began to reign; he reigned eight years in Jerusalem. He did not do what was pleasing before God, for he sacrificed at the altar of devils, and he died in his heathen practices.

NOTE.--In the Book of Adam he is called Aram. Zambri made war upon him, and he died denying God.

Ahaziah his son reigned after him, and he was twenty-two years old when [he began] to reign; he lived for one year in Jerusalem, and did evil things before God in that year. Because of the wickedness and iniquity which he wrought, God delivered him into the hands of his enemies and they killed him. When he was dead his mother [Athaliah] killed all the royal children of the house of David, imagining that she would uproot the children of the Jews. The only person of the seed of the royal house whom she did not slay was Joash, whom Yôshba` (Jehosheba), the daughter of Joram, the son of Jehosaphat, carried away secretly and hid [Fol. 33a, col. 1] with her in her house.

Reign of Ahab's sister

And the sister of Ahab reigned seven years in Jerusalem. And she polluted the city with fornication, for she commanded the women to play the whore without fear, and the men to commit adultery with the wives of their neighbours without incurring any penalty. And she herself committed fornication like Jezebel, and she adopted all the heathen practices of the house of Ahab in Jerusalem.

Reign of Joash

And after seven years the children of Jerusalem considered whom they should make their king, and Jehoiada the priest gathered them together in the house of the Lord, in the temple which Solomon had built. And when the captains of thousands and the captains of hundreds had gathered together, Jehoiada the priest said unto them, "Whom say ye shall be king and sit upon the throne of David except [he be] a king and the son of a king?" And when he showed him [Fol. 33a, col. 2] to them they rejoiced with an exceedingly great joy. And the captains of thousands, and the captains of hundreds, and the "runners," and the messengers brought the kingdom to the house of the Lord, and the soldiers who were armed surrounded him on all sides; and Jehoiada the priest set him (i.e. Joash) upon the throne of David his father. And [Joash] was seven years old when [he began] to reign, and he reigned forty years in Jerusalem. And the name of his mother was Sûbhâ (Zibea) and she was from Beersheba. And Athaliah [the mother of Ahaziah] was killed. And Joash requited with evil the kindness which Jehoiada had done him, and after his death he shed the innocent blood of his sons. And Joash died, and Amaziah his son reigned after him.

Amaziah was twenty-five years old when he began to reign, and he reigned twenty-nine years in Jerusalem; and the name of his mother was Yâhô`adhân (Joadan). And Amaziah died, and [Fol. 33b, col. 1] Uzziah his son reigned after him.

Uzziah was sixteen years old when [he began] to reign, and he reigned fifty (sic) years in Jerusalem; and the name of his mother was Îkhânyâ (Jechalia). And he did that which was good before the Lord. Now, he made bold to go into the Holy of Holies, and he took the censer from the priest of God (Azariah), and burned incense in the temple of the Lord; and because he did this leprosy covered his face. And because Isaiah the prophet did not rebuke him, he was prevented from prophesying until Uzziah died. And Jotham his son reigned in his stead.

Jotham was twenty-five years old when [he began] to reign, and he reigned sixteen years in Jerusalem; and the name of his mother was Îrûshâ (Jerusa), the daughter of Zadok. And he did that which was good before the Lord, and he died and Ahaz his son reigned after him.

Ahaz a vassal of the King of Assyria

Ahaz was twenty years old when [he began] to reign, and he reigned sixteen years in Jerusalem [Fol. 33b, col. 2]; and the name of his mother was `Aphin, the daughter of Levi. And he did that which was evil before the Lord, and he sacrificed to devils. Tiglath-Pileser, the king of Assyria, went up against him, and Ahaz wrote himself down in his letter as his servant, and the Assyrian held him in subjection. And Ahaz sent to the king of Assyria the gold and silver [which were in] the house of the Lord, [and in his days] the children of Israel were carried off into captivity. And the king sent for the men who had come from Babel, so that they might dwell in the land instead of the children of Israel, because they could kill the lions. And the king of Assyria sent to them Ôrî [Fol. 34a, col. 1] the priest, and he taught them the laws. And Ahaz died and Hezekiah his son reigned after him.

NOTE.--The Assyrian king who conquered Ahaz was Tiglath Pileser III, who reigned from 745-727 B.C. In a list of the kings in the British Museum which were his tributaries we find—

la-   u-   kha-   Zi   (matu)   la-   u-   da-   ai

Ahaz [king of] the country of the Judeans.

(Brit. Mus. K. 2751.)

Tiglath Pileser's Babylonian name was PU-LU, , which we find in the Bible under the form of "Pul." (See II Kings xv. 29; xvi. 7, 10; and I Chron. v. 26.)

Hezekiah

Hezekiah was twenty-five years old when [he began] to reign, and he reigned twenty-nine years in Jerusalem; and the name of his mother was Akhi (Abhi ?), the daughter of Zechariah. And he did that which was pleasing before the Lord, for he smashed the altars, and he cut in pieces the serpent of brass which Moses made in the wilderness, because the children of Israel used to worship it, and he abolished heathen practices in Jerusalem.

In the fourth year of his reign, Shalmaneser, king of Assyria, came up and carried away captive the rest of the children of Israel, and he sent them into Media, beyond Babel.

NOTE.--Tiglath Pileser III having conquered Syria carried away into captivity the Israelitish tribes of Reuben and Gad, and the half tribe of Manasseh. His successor Shelmaneser V, 𒀭 𒍧 ⟨ (727-722 B.C.) attacked Hosea, king of Israel, and conquered him and, because he was an ally of the king of Egypt, carried him off into captivity.

And in the twentieth year of Hezekiah, Sennacherib, king of Assyria, came up and took all the cities and towns of Judah, but through the prayer of Hezekiah Jerusalem was saved.

NOTE.--Sennacherib, 𒀭 𒉌 𒈾, king of Assyria, 705-681 B.C., having brought Padi from Jerusalem and made him king of Ekron, then marched on to attack

Kha-	za-	ki-	a-	u-	(matu) Ia-	u-	da-	ai

"Hezekiah [king of] the country of the Judeans."

He captured 46 of Hezekiah's strongholds, and brought out from them 200,150 people, and horses, mules, asses, camels, oxen, and innumerable sheep. He then shut up Hezekiah like a caged bird in

Ur-	sa-	li-	im-	mu	ali	sharru-	ti-	su

"Jerusalem the city of his sovereignty."

Hezekiah's soldiers deserted, and he sent his envoy to Nineveh to pay his tribute to Sennacherib, viz. 30 talents of gold, 800 talents of silver, precious stones, eye-paint, couches and chairs of ivory, hides, tusks, precious woods, and his daughters with their attendants and musicians.]

And Hezekiah became sick unto death [Fol. 34a, col. 2], and it was grievous unto him, and he wept. And there were certain men who blamed him, but why [his sickness] was grievous unto him they never troubled to acquaint themselves. Now the sorrow of Hezekiah [came upon him] because when he became sick unto death he had no son to reign after him. And when he looked with the eyes of his soul and saw that he had no son to reign after him, he was afflicted, and wept and said, "Woe is me! for I must die childless, and that blessing which hath been given [unto us] for six and forty generations hath been cut off by me this day. I have become the destroyer of the kingdom of David, and the succession of the kings of Judah hath been cut off this day." This was [the cause of] the sorrow of Hezekiah. And after he recovered from his sickness he waited fourteen years, and [then] Manasseh was born to him. And Hezekiah died in great content, and left a son to sit upon the throne of David [Fol. 34b, col. 1] his father.

Manasseh

Manasseh was twelve years old when [he began] to reign, and he reigned fifty-five years in Jerusalem; and the name of his mother was Habhsîbhâh (Hephziba). He was a man who was more evil and iniquitous than all those who had lived before him; he builded altars to devils, and sacrificed to idols, and he filled Jerusalem with iniquity and provoked God to wrath. And because Isaiah the prophet rebuked him, he threatened him and sent men who were sons of iniquity, and they sawed Isaiah the prophet in twain with a saw between [two pieces of] wood, from his head downwards to his feet. And Isaiah was one hundred and twenty years old when they sawed him in twain, and he had been the prophet of God for ninety years. And Manasseh repented after he had slain Isaiah, and he put sackcloth on his body, and decreed fasting for himself, and he ate bread with tears all the days of his life because he had committed iniquity and had [Fol. 34b, col. 2] slain the prophet. And Manasseh died, and Ammon reigned after him.

Ammon was twenty-two years old when [he began] to reign, and he reigned two years in Jerusalem; and the name of his mother was Mashlemath. And Ammon did evil before the Lord, and he made his sons to pass through fire; he died, and Josiah his son reigned after him. Josiah was eight years old when he began to reign, and he reigned thirty-one years in Jerusalem; and the name of his mother was Yadhîdhâ (Jedida), the daughter of Azariah (Adaja ?), from Bezkath. And he did what was good before the Lord, and he walked in all the way wherein his father David had walked; and he turned aside neither to the right hand nor to the left. And

Pharaoh, the "Lame" (i.e. Necho II) killed him, and Jehoahaz his son reigned after him.

NOTE.--Pharaoh Necho, king of Egypt 609-593 B.C., was the second king of the XXVIth Dynasty. His names as "King of the South and North" and "Son of Ra" are

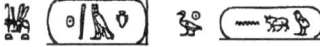

Uhem-a{dot-over}b-R‾a   N-Ka-u.

Jehoahaz was twenty-three years old when [he began] to reign, and he reigned three months in Jerusalem; and the name of his mother was Hamtâl, the daughter of [Fol. 35a, col. 1] Jeremiah from Lebhnâ. And he did what was evil before the Lord, even as Manasseh had done. And Pharaoh, the Lame, king of Egypt, took him prisoner in Diblath, in the land of Hamath, whilst he was king in Jerusalem, and he laid tribute on the land, one hundred talents of silver and ten talents of gold. And Pharaoh, the Lame, made Eliakim, the son of Jonah, king instead of Josiah his father, and he made his name to be Jehoiakim. And he carried away Jehoahaz, and he went to Egypt and died there. And Jehoiakim gave silver and gold to Pharaoh; he laid [the payment] of silver and gold on the land according to the word (i.e. command) of Pharoh's mouth. Every man, according to what it was right for him [to pay], brought silver and gold from the people of the land, according to the command of the mouth of Pharaoh, the Lame.

Jehoiakim was twenty-five years old when [he began] to reign, and he reigned eleven [Fol. 35a, col. 2] years in Jerusalem; and the name of his mother was Zebhîdhâ, the daughter of Pedâyâ, from Ramah. And he did that which was evil before the Lord, even as his fathers had done. In his days Nebuchadnezzar, king of Babel, went up against Jerusalem, and Jehoiakim became his vassal for three years. Then he turned and rebelled against him, and the Lord stirred up bands of robbers against him because of his sins. And Jehoiakim slept with his fathers, and Jehoiachin his son reigned after him. And the king of Egypt did not come forth again out of his country; for the king of Babel captured all the land that belonged to the king of Egypt, from the river of Egypt to the river Euphrates.

Jehoiachin was eighteen years old when [he began] to reign, and he reigned three months in Jerusalem; and the name of his mother was Neheshtâ, the daughter of Elyâthân (Elnathan ?), from Jerusalem. And he did that which was evil before the [Fol. 35b, col. 1] Lord, even as his father had done. At that time Nebuchadnezzar, king of Babel, went up against Jerusalem, and the king of Babel took him with him in the eighth year of his kingdom. And he brought out from there all the treasure of the house of the Lord, and the treasure of the king' s house, and he carried off into captivity to Babel all [the people of] Jerusalem, and Jehoiachin, and his mother, and his wives, and his nobles; and the king brought captive to Babel all the men who had made war. And the king of Babel made Methanyâ, the uncle [of Jehoiachin] king in his stead, and he called his name "Zedekiah."

The Capture of Jerusalem

Zedekiah was twenty years old when [he began] to reign, and he reigned eleven years in Jerusalem; and the name of his mother was Hamtâl, the daughter of Jeremiah, from Libnah. And he did that which was evil before the Lord, even as did Jehoiakim, and the wrath of the [Fol. 35b, col. 2] Lord was (i.e. fell upon) Jerusalem. And Zedekiah rebelled against the king of Babel, and in the ninth year of his kingdom Nebuchadnezzar, king of Babel, came against Jerusalem, and the city was fettered with affliction (i.e. besieged) until the eleventh year of king Zedekiah. And the city was rent open (i.e. its wall was breached), and all the mighty men of war fled from the city by night by way of the plain. And the soldiers of the Chaldeans pursued the king, and they overtook him on the plain of Jericho, and all his soldiers were driven away from him; and the Chaldeans captured Zedekiah and took him up to the king of Babel at Debhlath (Riblah), and he passed judgment upon him. And the king of Babel slew the sons of Zedekiah the king before his eyes, and he blinded the eyes of Zedekiah, and bound him in chains, and carried him to Babel [Fol. 36a, col. 1]. And Simeon the high priest, because he had freedom of speech with the commander of the [Chaldean] army, made entreaty to him, and the commander of the army gave him all the books of the Scriptures and did not burn them; and Simeon the high priest gathered them together and cast them into a pit (or dry well). And Jerusalem was laid waste and made desolate, and no man remained therein except Jeremiah, the Prophet, who sat and raised lamentations over it for twenty years. And Jeremiah, the Prophet, died in Samaria, and the priest Ûr buried him in Jerusalem, according to the oath which the prophet made him to swear.

Now up to the time of the destruction of Jerusalem the Hebrew, Greek, and Syrian writers were in possession of the truth, and they were able to produce the registers of the genealogies of the tribes and the people. But from the destruction of Jerusalem and onwards there has been no truth in their writings, except as regards the heads of the tribes (i.e. the Patriarchs) [Fol. 36a, col. 2], and they are unable to prove whence the succession of the priests took its origin.

Jehoiachin

And Jehoiachin was bound in prison for thirty-seven years, and after he came forth from prison he took to wife Gûlîth, the daughter of Eliakim, and he begot by her in Babel Shalathiel (Salathiel); and Jehoiachin died in Babel. And Salathiel took to wife Hetbath, the daughter of Halkânâ, and he begot by her Zûrbâbhel (Zerubbabel), who took to wife Malkath, the daughter of Ezra the scribe; but no son was born to him by her in Babel. In the days of Zerubbabel, the prince of Judah, Cyrus the Persian reigned in Babel. [A reproduction of a sculptured relief of Cyrus is given on Plate I. The official account of his conquest of Babylon is found on a baked clay cylinder now in the British Museum. See Plate II.]

Cyrus

And Cyrus took to wife the daughter of Salathiel, the sister of Zerubbabel, and he took her to wife according to the law of the Persians, and made her [his] queen. And she entreated Cyrus to bring about the return of the children of Israel [to Jerusalem]. And inasmuch as Zerubbabel was her brother, she was very insistent about [Fol. 36b, col. 1] the return [to Jerusalem] of those who had been led away into captivity. Now Cyrus loved his wife as he loved himself, and he did for her what she wished. And he sent forth heralds into all the land of Babel, ordering all the children of Israel to gather themselves together. And when they were gathered together Cyrus said unto Zerubbabel, his wife's brother, "Rise up, and take with thee all the children of thy people, and go up to Jerusalem in peace; and [re]build the city of thy fathers, and dwell and reign therein. And because Cyrus brought about the return of the children of Israel [to Jerusalem], God said, "I have taken my servant Cyrus by his right hand" (Isa. xliv. 28; xlv. 1). And the name of Cyrus was called "My shepherd, the anointed of the Lord," because his seed was received into the seed of David through Meshayyanath, the sister of Zerubbabel, whom he had taken to wife. And the children of Israel went up from Babel, and Zerubbabel became king over them; and Joshua, the son of Yôzâdâk, the son of Aaron, was high priest, even as the angel showed Zechariah the prophet, and said unto him, "These are the sons of the oil of consecration."

THE FIVE HUNDRED YEARS FROM THE SECOND YEAR OF CYRUS TO THE BIRTH OF CHRIST

NOW when the people had gone up [to Jerusalem] they had no Books of the Prophets. And Ezra the scribe went down into that pit [wherein Simeon had cast the Books], and he found a censer full of fire, and the perfume of the incense which rose up from it. And thrice he took some of the dust of those Books, and cast it into his mouth, and straightway God made to abide in him the spirit of prophecy, and he renewed all the Books of the Prophets.

NOTE.--According to the Book of Adam (iv. 10) the manuscripts and the library of the Temple were burnt. Simeon begged the commander to give him the ruins of the library, and he went in and collected the ashes of the books and put them into a pot, which he placed in a vault. He filled a censer with coals and incense, and, having lighted the fire, he set the censer over the place where the ashes of the books lay. The fire continued to burn until Ezra came to the vault, and the smoke of the incense was rising from the censer. He spread his hands thrice over the ashes of the books, and God gave him the spirt of prophecy, and he rewrote the Books of the Law and the Prophets.

And that same fire which was found in the pit became the holy fire in the house of the Lord. And Zerubbabel reigned in Jerusalem, and Joshua, the son of Yôzâdâk, was high-priest, and Ezra was the scribe of the Law and the Prophets. And the children of Israel [Fol. 37a, col. 1] celebrated a Passover when they went up from Babel. These are the three Passovers which the children of Israel kept; the first was [kept] in Egypt in the days of Moses; the the second was [kept] in the reign of Josiah; the third was [kept] when they went up from the land of Babel. And now an end hath been made to the Passover for them for ever. From the first captivity of Jerusalem, that in which Daniel went down into captivity, to the reign of Cyrus the Persian, was seventy years according to the prophecy of Jeremiah. And the children of Israel began the [re]building of the Temple in the days of Zerubbabel, and Joshua, the son of Yôzâdôk, and Ezra the scribe, and the building thereof was finished in six and forty years, even as it is written in the holy Gospel (John ii. 19).

The genealogies of the later Israelites

Now the genealogy of the tribes (or, families) was lost by [Fol. 37a, col. 2] the scribes, and they were unable to show either whence the heads of families took [their] wives, or whence they came. I, however, possess the knowledge of the correct genealogy, and will show the truth to everyman. When the children of Israel went up from Babylon--

Zerubbabel begot Abiud by Malkath, the daughter of Ezra the scribe.
Abiud took to wife Zakhyath, the daughter of Joshua, the son of Yôzâdâk, the priest, and begot by her Eliakim.
Eliakim took to wife Hâlâbh, the daughter of Dôrnîbh, and begot by her `Azôr.
`Azôr took to wife Yalpath, the daughter of Hazôr, and begot by her Zadok.
Zadok took to wife Kaltîn, the daughter of Dôrnibh, and begot by her Akhîn.
Akhîn took to wife Heskath, the daughter of Ta`îl, and begot by her Eliud.
Eliud took to wife Beshtîn, the daughter of [Fol. 37b, col. 1] Hasâl, and begot by her Eleazar.
Eleazar took to wife Dîbath, the daughter of Tôlâh, and begot by her Mâtthân.
Mâtthân took to wife Sebhrath, the daughter of Phinehas, and begot by her two sons at one conception, Jacob and Yônâkhîr.
Jacob took to wife Hadbhîth, the daughter of Eleazur, and begot by her Joseph.
Yônakhîr took Dînâ, the daughter of Pâkôdh, and begot by her Mary, of whom was born the Christ.

And because none of the early writers could discover the order of succession of the generations of their fathers, the Jews urged the sons of the Church very strongly to show them [who were] the fathers of the blessed Mary in the order of the succession of their families. And they pressed the children of the Church to enquire into the genealogy of the families [Fol. 37b, col. 2] of their fathers, and to show them the truth. For the Jews call Mary an adulteress. And here the mouth of the Jews is stopped, and they believe that Mary was of the seed of the house of David and of Abraham. Now the Jews have no table of succession which showeth them the true order of the families of their fathers, because their books have been burned thrice--once in the days of Antiochus [IV. Epiphanes], who raised up a persecution against them, and polluted the Temple of the Lord, and forced them to offer up sacrifices unto idols; the second time in the days of . . . . ; and the third time in the days of Herod, when Jerusalem was destroyed. Because of this the Jews were greatly grieved, for they had no trustworthy table of the succession of the generations of their fathers. And they toiled eagerly [Fol. 38a, col. 1] that they might obtain the truth, but they were unable to do so.

Now the Jews had many writers, and each of them wrote what he pleased, and no two of them agreed in what they wrote, because they could not stand on a foundation of truth. And even our own writers, the children of the Church, cannot show us the certainty of the real truth. They cannot show how the ascent of the body of Adam to Golgotha took place, nor whence came the fathers (or, ancestors) of Melchisedek, and the fathers of the blessed woman Mary. And the children of Israel being urged by the Church, and being unable to ascertain the truth, waxed reckless, and wrote, as it were, in the madness of error. [Here the text is faulty and incomplete.] And as concerning the table of succession of the sixty-three families, which [reach] from Adam to Christ, the Greek writers, and the Hebrew writers, and the Syrian writers, can neither show whence each head of a family took his wife [Fol. 38a, col. 2], nor whose daughter she was. Now each divine doctor (or, teacher) has laid down for the Church one true doctrine, and they have given unto believers the armour wherewith they can fight and overcome her enemies. Besides this, the grace of Christ hath granted unto us that which was lacking in them, and this we will cast into the rich treasury [of their knowledge]. And this, with great diligence, we have bestirred ourselves to do, even as our truly loving brother in Christ, the illustrious Nâmôsâyâ (Nemesius ?) greatly desireth. And although I have been hindered through my dilatoriness, thou hast through thy love of learning, not been dilatory. And because of thy loving kindness towards me, and also because I myself am eager not to withhold from thee that which thou requirest of me, I will [here] write down [Fol. 38b, col. 1] the true table of succession. Hear, O my brother Nemesius (?) the following table of succession which I write for thee; none of the [other] doctors hath been able to light upon it. The following are the sixty-three generations from which the Incarnation of Christ is descended, and their order is thus:--

1. Adam begot Seth.

2. Seth took to wife Kelîmath, who was born with Abel, and begot by her Enos.

3. Enos took to wife Hannâ, the daughter of Jubal, the daughter of Hôh, the daughter of Seth, and begot by her Cainan.

4. Cainan took to wife Peryath, the daughter of Kôtûn, the daughter of Yarbâl, and begot by her Mahlâlâîl.

5. Mahlâlâîl took to wife Sehatpar, the daughter of Enos, and begot by her Yârêd (Jared).

6. Jared took to wife Zebhîdhâ, the daughter of Kuhlôn, the daughter of Kenan, and begot by her Enoch.

7. Enoch took to wife Zadhkîn, the daughter of Tôpîh, the daughter of Mahlâlâîl, and begot by her Methuselah.

8. Methuselah took to wife Sâkhûth, the daughter of Sôkhîn, and begot by her Lamech.

9. Lamech took to wife Kîpâr, the daughter of Tûthâth, the daughter of Methuselah, and begot by her Noah.

10. Noah took to wife Haykâl, the daughter of Namûs, and he begot by her Shem, Ham and Japhet.

11. Shem begot Arpakhshar (Arphaxad) .

12. Arphaxad begot Shâlâh (Salah).

13. Salah begot Âbhâr (Eber).

14. Eber begot Pâlâg (Peleg) .

15. Peleg begot Ar`ô (Reu) .

16. Reu begot Sârôgh (Serug) .

17. Serug took to wife Kâhâl, the daughter of Peleg, who begot Nâhôr.

18. Nâhôr took to wife Napûsh (Yapûsh ?), the daughter of Reu, and begot Tarah (Terah).

19. Terah took two wives, Yônâ and Salmûth; by Yônâ he begot Abraham, and by Salmûth he begot Sârâ (Sarah) [Fol. 39a, col. 1].

20. Abraham took to wife Sarah and begot Isaac.

21. Isaac took to wife Rebecca and begot Jacob.

22. Jacob took to wife Leah and begot Judah.

23. Judah begot Pars (Pharez) by Tamar.

24. Pharez begot Hezron.

25. Hezron begot Aram.

26. Aram begot Amminadab.

27. Amminadab begot Nahshôn (Nahasson).

28. Nahasson begot Salmon.

29. Salmon begot Boaz, by Rahab.

30. Boaz took to wife Ruth, the daughter of Lot, and begot Obed.

31. Obed begot Jesse.
32. Jesse begot David the king.
33. David took to wife Bathsheba, and begot by her Solomon.
34. Solomon begot Rehoboam.
35. Rehoboam begot Abijah.
36. Abijah begot Asa.
37. Asa begot Jehoshaphat.
38. Jehoshaphat begot Joram [Fol. 39a, col. 2].
39. Joram begot Ahaziah.
40. Ahaziah begot Joash.
41. Joash begot Amaziah.
42. Amaziah begot Uzziah.
43. Uzziah begot Jotham.
44. Jotham begot Ahaz.
45. Ahaz begot Hezekiah.
46. Hezekiah begot Manasseh.
47. Manasseh begot Amon.
48. Amon begot Josiah.
49. Josiah begot Jehoiakim.
50. Jehoiakim begot Jehoiachin.
51. Jehoiachin begot Salathiel.
52. Salathiel begot Nedabijah (sic).
53. Nedabijah begot Zerubbabel.
54. Zerubbabel begot Abiud.
55. Abiud begot Eliakim.
56. Eliakim begot Azor.
57. Azor begot Zadok.
58. Zadok begot Achin.
59. Achin begot Eliud.
60. Eliud begot Eleazar.
61. Eleazar begot Mâtthan.
62. Mâtthan took to wife Sabhrath, the daughter of Phinehas, and begot Jacob and Yônâkhîr.
63. Jacob took to wife Hadhbhîth, the daughter of Eleazar, and begot Joseph, the betrothed of Mary [Fol. 39b, col. 1].

Yônâkhîr took to wife Dînâ, that is to say, Hannâ, the daughter of Pâkôdh, and sixty years after he had taken her to wife she brought forth Mary, of whom was born Christ.

The Genealogy of Mary

And because Joseph was the son of Mary's uncle, by the fore-knowledge of God, Who knew that Mary would be certainly attacked by the Jews, Mary was given to Joseph, who was the son of her uncle, that he might take care of her. Observe, O our brother Nemesius, that the fathers of the blessed woman Mary belonged to the succession of the generations of David.

NOTE.--An alternative genealogy is given in the Book of the Bee (chapter xxxiii), and reads: David begot Nathan, Nathan begot Mattatha, Mattatha begot Mani, Mani begot Melea, Melea begot Eliakim, Eliakim begot Jonam, Jonam begot Levi. [Add Joseph, Juda and Simeon from Luke iii. 19, 20.] Levi begot Mattîtha, Mattîtha begot Jorim, Jorim begot Eliezer, Eliezer begot Jose, Jose begot Er. Er begot Elmodad, Elmodad begot Cosam, Cosam begot Addi, Addi begot Melchi, Melchi begot Neri, Neri begot Salathiel, Salathiel begot Zerubbabel, Zerubbabel begot Rhesa, Rhesa begot Johannan, Johannan begot Juda, Juda begot Joseph, Joseph begot Semei, Semei begot Mattatha, Mattatha begot Maath, Maath begot Nagge, Nagge begot Esli, Esli begot Nahum, Nahum begot Amos, Amos begot Mattîtha, Mattîtha begot Joseph, Joseph begot Janni, Janni begot Melchi, Melchi begot Levi, Levi begot Matthat, Matthat begot Heli, Heli begot Joseph.

Behold, I have set thee upon a foundation of truth, which none of the [former] chroniclers found to stand upon; see, too, how these sixty-three generations [reaching] from Adam to the birth of Christ, succeeded each other. And the Jews also rejoiced [Fol. 39b, col. 2] because they also had found the generations of the familles of their fathers.

Observe, O our brother Nemesius, that in the days of Cyrus the FIFTH THOUSAND [YEARS] CAME TO AN END. And from the thousand [years] of Cyrus until the Passion of our Redeemer, the years were in number five hundred, according to the prophecy of Daniel, who prophesied and said, "After sixty-two weeks the Messiah shall be slain." And these weeks make five hundred years.

NOTE.--According to the Book of Adam (iv. 14), Daniel said, "After seven weeks Christ shall come, and shall be put to death." Now seven weeks are 490 years, for a great week contains 70 years. But on that the prophet said, "after seven years," he pointed to the [remaining] ten [of the 500 years].

Daniel did not say, "Christ shall come at the end of seven weeks," but "after seven weeks, and He shall be put to death."

Behold, from this time the mouth of the Jews is shut, for they have dared to say that the Messiah hath not yet come. They must, perforce, do one of two things: either accept the prophecy of Daniel, or say, "We do not accept it." For the prophecy hath fulfilled itself, and the weeks have passed, and the Messiah hath been slain, and the Holy City hath been laid waste by Vespasian.

The Birth of Christ

Observe now [Fol. 40a, col. 1], O thou lover of learning, our brother Nemesius, in the forty-second year of the kingdom of Augustus, Christ was born in Bethlehem of Judah, as it is written in the Holy Gospel.

The Star and the Magi

Now, it was two years before Christ was born that the star appeared to the Magi. They saw the star in the firmament of heaven, and the brilliancy of its appearance was brighter than that of every other star. And within it was a maiden carrying a child, and a crown was set upon his head. Now it was the custom of the ancient kings, and the Magi of the Chaldeans, to consult the Signs of the Zodiac about all the affairs of their lives. And when the Magi saw the star they were perturbed, and terrified, and afraid, and the whole land of Persia was disturbed. And the kings, and the Magi, and the Chaldeans [Fol. 40a, col. 2], and the wise men of Persia, were stupefied, and they were exceedingly afraid of the portent which they saw. And they said, "Peradventure the king of the Greeks hath determined to wage war against the land of Nimrod." And the Magi and the Chaldeans were terrified, and they consulted their books of wisdom, and through the might of the wisdom of their books they understood and learned, and stood upon the strength of the truth. Now, in truth, the Magi of the Chaldeans discovered that by means of the motions of the stars, to which they gave the name of "Signs of the Zodiac," they were able to know and understand the strength (or, importance) of events before they took place. And this same knowledge is also given to those who go down into the sea, and by the motions of the stars they know beforehand when there is going to be a disturbance of the winds, and when a violent storm is going to rise up against them, and whenever they are about to be threatened with danger from winds and waves. Thus also was it with the Magi. When they saw and read in the [Fol. 40b, col. 1] "Revelation of Nimrod" they discovered therein that a king was born in Judah, and the whole path of the Dispensation of Christ was revealed unto them.

NOTE.--As touching the nature of that star, whether it was a star in its nature, or in appearance only, it is right to know that it was not of the other stars, but a secret power which appeared like a star; for all the other stars that are in the firmament, and the sun and moon, perform their course from east to west. This one, however, made its course from north to south, for Palestine lies thus, over against Persia. This star was not seen by them at night only, but also during the day, and at noon; and it was seen at the time when the sun is particularly strong, because it was not one of the stars. Now the moon is stronger in its light than all the stars, but it is immediately quenched and its light dissipated by one small ray of the sun. But this star overcame even the beams of the sun by the intensity of its light. Sometimes it appeared, and sometimes it was hidden entirely. It guided the Magi as far as Palestine. . . . . . This was not an ordinary movement of the stars, but a rational power. Moreover, it had no fixed path. It did not remain always in the height of heaven, but sometimes it came down, and sometimes it mounted up. Book of the Bee (chapter xxxviii).

The Signs of the Zodiac

The names of the Babylonian Signs of the Zodiac were:--

1   𒀯 𒈜 𒀊 𒄖
(amel) Agru

2   𒀯 𒀯 𒀯 𒇀 𒈝 𒄖
Kakkab u Alap shame

3   { 𒀯 𒉺 𒁉 𒄖 𒈝 𒁉
Re'u kinu shame u

      𒀯 𒈬 𒇀 𒈝 𒁉 𒁉
Tu'ame rabuti

4   𒀯 𒄖 𒁉

AL.LUL (Shittu ?)

5　　　𒀯　　(cuneiform signs)

Kalbu rabu

6　　　𒀯　　(cuneiform signs)

Shiru

7　　　𒀯　　(cuneiform signs)

Zibanitum

8　　　𒀯　　(cuneiform signs)

Akrabu

9　　　𒀯　　(cuneiform signs)

PA-BIL-SAG

10　　　𒀯　　(cuneiform signs)

SUḪUR.MASH

11　　　𒀯　　(cuneiform signs)

Gula

12　　　𒀯　　(cuneiform signs)

DILGANU u Rikis nuni

(The sign placed before each name is the determinative for star.)

	Meaning of the name.	Modern equivalent.	Name of month.	
1	The Labourer	Goat	Nisannu	(cuneiform)
2	The Star and the Bull of heaven	Bull	Airu	(cuneiform)
3	The Faithful Shepherd of heaven and the Great Twins	Twins	Simanu	(cuneiform)
4	The Tortoise	Crab	Duuzu	(cuneiform)
5	The Great Dog (Lion)	Lion	Abu	(cuneiform)
6	Virgin with ear of corn	Virgin	Ululu	(cuneiform)

7		Scales	Tashritum	⟨𒉎⟩
8	The Scorpion	Scorpion	Ara<u>h</u> shamna	𒀀
9	Enurta (the god)	Bow	Kislimu	𒆠
10	The Goat-fish	Capricornus	<u>T</u>ebetum	𒈾
11	The Great Star	Water-Bearer	Shabatu	𒋛
12	The star . . . and the Band of Fishes	The Fishes	Addaru	𒌋

On the first Zodiac which was set up by Tiâmat, the Evil one, see The Babylonian Legends of the Creation, London, 1921, page 17 (British Museum publication.)]

And straightway, according to what they had received from the tradition which had been handed down to them by their fathers, they left the East, and went up to the mountains of Nôdh, which lie inside the entrances to the East from the lands on the skirts of the North, and they took from them gold, and myrrh, and frankincense. And from this [passage] understand, O my brother Nemesius, that the Magi knew the whole service of the Dispensation of our Redeemer through the offerings which they brought: the gold was for a king, the myrrh for a physician, and the frankincense for a priest, for the Magi knew Who He was, and that He was a king, and a physician, and a priest. Now when the son of the king of Sheba was a little boy his father brought him [Fol. 40b, col. 2] to a Rabbi, and he learned the Book of the Hebrews better than all his companions and his fellow countrymen, and he said unto all his slaves, "It is written in all the books of genealogies that the king shall be born in Bethlehem."

The names of the Magi

These are they who bore offerings to the King, kings, the sons of kings:--

1. HÔRMÎZDADH of Mâkhôzdî, king of Persia, who was called "King of Kings," and dwelt in Lower Âdhôrghîn.
2. ÎZGARAD (Yazdegerd), the king of Sâbhâ.
3. PERÔZÂDH, the king of Sheba, which is in the East.

NOTE.--In the Book of Adam (iv. 15) the kings are called Hor, king of Persia, Basantar, king of Saba, and Karsundas, king of the East. According to the Book of the Bee (chapter xxxix), the Magi were twelve in number, and their names were:--

Zarwândâd, the son of Artabân.
Hôrmîzdâd, the son of Sîtârûk (Santarôk).
Gûshnâsâph (Gushnasp), the son of Gûndaphar.
Arshakh, the son of Mîhârôk.
These four brought gold.
Zarwândâd, the son of Wârzwâd.
Îryâhô, the son of Kesro (Khusrau).
Artahshesht, the son of Holîtî.
Ashtôn`âbôdân, the son of Shîshrôn.
These four brought myrrh.
Mehârôk, the son of Hûhâm.
Ahshiresh, the son of Hasbân.
Sardâlâh, the son of Baladân.
Merôdâch, the son of Beldarân.
These four brought frankincense.

The Magi in Jerusalem

And the Magi having made ready to go up, the kingdom of the mighty men of war was perturbed and terrified, and there was with the Magi so mighty a following that all the cities of the East were in dismay before them, and Jerusalem also. And when they entered the presence of Herod, he trembled before them, and he commanded them, saying, "Depart in [Fol. 41a, col. 1] peace, and seek diligently for the young Child, and when ye have found Him, come and show me, that I too may go and make obeisance unto Him"; though deceit was hidden in Herod's heart, he offered homage with his mouth. Now when, the Magi went up to Jerusalem there was great commotion in Judea, because of the edict of Augustus Cæsar, which commanded that every man should be registered in his country, and in the city of his fathers. Because of this Herod was greatly perturbed, and he said unto the Magi, "Go ye and search for Him." Now the Magi are called "Magi" because of the garb of Magianism in which the heathen kings arrayed themselves whensoever they offered up a sacrifice and made offerings to their gods. They made use of two different kinds of apparel; that which appertained to royalty [they wore] inside, and that which appertained to Magianism outside [Fol. 41a, col. 2]. And thus also was it with those who went up prepared to make offerings to Christ, and they were arrayed in both kinds of apparel.

And when the Magi had gone forth from Jerusalem, and from the presence of Herod, that same star which had been their guide on the road appeared to them, and they rejoiced greatly. And the star went on before them until they entered the cave, where they saw the young Child swathed in bands and laid in a manger. Whilst they were on their way up thither they said within themselves, "When we arrive there we shall see mighty and wonderful things, according to the law and custom which prevail among royal personages when a king is born." Thus did they think that they would find in the land of Israel a royal palace, and couches of gold with cushions laid upon them [Fol. 41b, col. 1], and the king and the son of the king arrayed in purple, and awestruck soldiers and companies of royal troops, and the nobles of the kingdom paying him honour by presenting gifts, and tables laid out with meats fit for the king, and vessels of drink standing in rows, and men servants and women servants serving in fear. Such were the things which the Magi expected to see, but they saw them not; they saw sights which were far better than these when they went into the cave. They saw Joseph sitting in astonishment, and Mary in a state of wonderment, but there was no couch with cushions laid upon it, and no table with food laid out upon it, and no sign of the preparations which accompany royal state. And although they saw all this humble estate and poverty, they had no doubt in their minds, but they drew nigh in fear and made obeisance to Him in honour, and they offered [Fol. 41b, col. 2] unto Him, gold, and myrrh, and frankincense. And it was very grievous unto Mary and Joseph that they had nothing to set before them, but the Magi fed themselves with food of their own providing.

NOTES.--In addition to the gold, frankincense and myrrh which the Magi brought, they laid before the Child as an offering thirty zûzê of silver. Their weight was according to the weight of the sanctuary, but they were equal to six hundred pieces according to the weight of the country. (The Syriac zûzê = the Arabic dirham and the Greek drachme.) The thirty pieces were made by Terah, who gave them to Abraham, who gave them to Isaac. With them Isaac bought a village, and the man who received them took them to Pharaoh. Pharaoh sent them to David as a contribution towards the building of the Temple, and Solomon placed them round the door of the altar. Nebuchadnezzar carried them away to Babylon, and gave them to certain royal Persian hostages, who took them to Persia and gave them to their parents. When the Magi set out for Jerusalem they took the thirty pieces with their other offerings out with them they bought from certain shepherds at Edessa "the garment without seam," which an angel had given to them. Abgar, king of Edessa, took the thirty pieces and the garment from the shepherds, and sent them to Christ. Christ kept the garment and sent the thirty pieces to the Jewish treasury. The priests gave them to Judas Iscariot for betraying our Lord, but he repented and took them back to the priests. After Judas hanged himself the priests purchased a burial ground for strangers with the thirty pieces (Book of the Bee, chapter xliv) . Another legend says that Joseph had the thirty pieces, and that with them he bought spices to embalm Jacob. They passed into the possession of the Queen of Sheba, who gave them to Solomon (Sandeys, Christmas Carols, London, 1883, page lxxxiii).

The Circumcision of Christ

Now Christ was eight days old when the Magi presented their offerings; and Mary received them at the very time when Joseph circumcised Christ. In truth, Joseph circumcised Him according to the Law, but he only went through (or imitated) the act of cutting, for no [flesh] whatsoever was cut off from Him. For as [a rod of] iron passeth through the fire and cutteth the rays thereof, without any part of it being cut off from it, so in like manner was Christ circumcised without anything being taken from Him.

The Conversion of the Magi

And the Magi lived with the Child three days, and they saw the hosts of heaven going up and coming down to Christ. And they heard the sound [Fol. 42a, col. 1] of the praises of the angels, who sang hymns and cried out, "Holy, Holy, Holy, Mighty God, with whose praises the heavens and the earth are filled." And they were in great fear, and in truth they believed in Christ, and said, "This is the King Who hath come down from heaven and become man." And Perôzdhâdh answered and said unto them, "Now know I that the prophecy of Isaiah is true. For when I was in the school of the Hebrews I read in [the Book of] Isaiah, and I found [written] therein thus: 'For unto us a child is born, and unto us a son hath been given. And His Name shall be called Wonderful, and Counsellor, and God, Giant of the Worlds'" (Isa. ix. 6). And it is written in another place, "Behold, a virgin is with child, and she shall bring forth a son, and his name shall be called

'Emmanuel,' which is, being interpreted, 'God with us'" (Isa. vii. 14). And because He became like a man, and the angels were coming down [Fol. 42a, col. 2] from heaven to Him, truly He is the Lord of angels and men. And all the Magi believed and said, "Truly this King is God. Kings are born unto us frequently, and mighty men, the sons of mighty men, are born unto us on earth, but it is an unheard-of thing for the angels to come down to them." And straightway they all rose up, and did homage to Him as the Lord and King of the world. And having prepared food for their journey, they went down to their own country by a desert road.

The Massacre of the Innocents

Now, there are certain men who will dispute this [statement] and say, "Where was Christ when the children were massacred, for it is written that He was not found in the land of Judah?" It was because of this massacre that He fled to Egypt, so that there might be fulfilled that which is written [Fol. 42b, col. 1]. "From Egypt I called my Son" (Hos. xi. 1). And know this also. When Christ entered Egypt all the idols therein were swept from their places, and fell down, and were broken, so that there might be fulfilled that which is written, "Behold, the Lord rideth on a swift cloud, and entereth Egypt, and the idols of Egypt shall be broken before Him" (Isa. xix. 1).

NOTE.--When Joseph and Mary and the Child reached the gate of the city of Hermopolis, there were by the two buttresses of the gate two figures of brass that had been made by the sages and philosophers; and they spoke like men. When our Lord entered Egypt these two figures cried out with a loud voice, saying, "A great king has come into Egypt." Book of the Bee (chapter xl.)

And He did not return from Egypt [at once], but lived there until Herod died, and after him reigned Archelaus.

Now, thou must know, O my brother Nemesius, that, even as I have already told thee, all the men who were under the rule of Herod were [included] in that registration for taxation; and the registration was completed in fifty days. And it was not until this registration was completed and sealed, and until Herod had sealed it and sent it to Augustus in Rome, that the Messiah was searched for; up to that time [Fol. 42b, col. 2] no children had been slain. And it was during the commotion caused by that registration that Christ was born. When forty days after His birth had been fulfilled, Christ went into the Temple of the Lord. And Simeon the Aged, the son of Joshua bar-Yôzâdhâk, in whose days the captivity went up from Babel, took Him in his arms. Now, Simeon was five hundred years old when he took Christ in his arms.

The Flight into Egypt.[4]

And straightway the angel said unto Joseph, "Arise, take the young Child and His mother, and flee into Egypt." And when the registration was completed, the Jews were dismissed, so that each man might depart to his own district and to his own village.

Herod and John the Baptist

Then did Herod enquire for the Magi, and when he was told, "they have gone back to their own country," he was exceedingly wroth, and he sent straightway and slew all the young children in Bethlehem, and in all the villages round about. And when Herod had passed among the [Fol. 43a, col. 1] slain children, and they did not find there [the body of] John, the son of Zacharias, he said, "Truly, his son will reign over Israel." For he had heard of what had been said unto Zacharias by the angel, when he announced to him concerning [the birth of] John. And Herod sent to Zacharias [and commanded him] to bring John, and Zacharias said, "I am a priest, and I minister in the Temple of the Lord; I do not know where the Child and his mother are." And because of these words Zacharias was slain between the bench (or, steps) and the altar. Now, Elizabeth had taken John and gone forth into the desert.

The Death of Herod

And as for Herod, a divine punishment that was pitiless overtook him, and he fell ill of a sickness through which he stank, and his body melted away into a mass of worms, and he suffered most grievous pains, and at length people were unable to come near him because of his putrid smell. And through that bitter suffering [Fol. 43a, col. 2] his soul departed into outer darkness. Nevertheless, by his death he destroyed many.

NOTE.--First of all, he slew his wife and his daughter, and he killed one man of every family, saying, "At the time of my death there shall be mourning and weeping and lamentation in the whole city." His bowels and his legs were swollen with running sores, and matter flowed from them, and he was consumed by worms. He had nine wives and thirteen children. There was a knife in his hand, and he was eating an apple; and by reason of the severity of his pain, he drew the knife across his throat, and cut it with his own hand; and his belly burst open, and he died and went to perdition. An evil fate also overtook Bôzîyâ, the daughter of Herodias, who begged for the head of John the Baptist on a charger. Having given the saint's head to her mother, she went out to dance upon the ice, but the ice broke and she sank into the water up to her neck, and no one could deliver her. At length men came with the sword which had been used in beheading John, and they cut off Bôzîyâ's head and gave it to her mother. The right hand with which Herodias took up John's head withered, and when she saw the heads of the saint and her daughter she became blind, and Satan entered her and bound her with fetters. See Book of the Bee (chapters xxxix and xli).

Now Herod had said unto Archelaus his son, and unto Shâlôm his sister, "Immediately I am dead, let those whom I have fettered in prison be slain"--now he had imprisoned one person from every house. And he said, "I know that the Jews will feel great joy at my death. But in order that they may not rejoice and be glad whilst ye are sorrowful and are weeping, let all those whom I have shut up in prison be slain, so that through their death they may cause lamentation unintentionally." And Archelaus and Shâlôm did as Herod commanded them, and when this order had been carried out in all Judea there remained not one house in which there was not lamentation, even as it was in Egypt [in days of old].

Christ returns to Galilee

And when Herod died, and his death had been announced to Joseph, he went back to Galilee. And when Christ was thirty years old [Fol. 43b, col. 1] He was baptized by John. Now John was in the desert all the days of his life, and he lived upon the root which is called "Kâmûs," which is wild honey. [According to some this root was like unto a carrot.] And in the twelfth year of the kingdom of Tiberius Christ suffered.

Chronological statement

Understand now and see, O my brother Nemesius, that in the days of Yârêd, in his fortieth year, the FIRST Thousand Years came to an end. In the six hundredth year of Noah the SECOND Thousand Years came to an end. In the seventy-fourth year of Reu the THIRD Thousand Years came to an end. In the twenty-sixth year of Âhôr (Ehud) the FOURTH Thousand Years came to an end. In the second year of Cyrus the FIFTH Thousand Years came to an end. And in the five hundredth year of the SIXTH Thousand Years Christ was born in His human form.

The Crucifixion of Christ

And know thou also that Christ dwelt [Fol. 43b, col. 2] in Mary, and suffered in Nazareth, and was born in Bethlehem, and was laid in a manger, and was carried by Simeon in the Temple of Solomon, and was reared in Galilee, and was anointed by Mary Magdalene, and ate the Passover in the house of Nicodemus, the brother of Joseph of Râmethâ, and was bound in the house of Hannân, and was struck with a reed in the house of Caiaphas, and embraced the pillar and was scourged with a whip in the Prætorium of Pilate, and on Friday, on the first day of Nîsân (April), on the fourteenth day of the moon, our Redeemer suffered.

At the FIRST HOUR of Friday God fashioned Adam from the dust, and at the first hour of Friday Christ received spittle from the sons of Adam.

At the SECOND HOUR of Friday the wild beasts, and the cattle, and the feathered fowl gathered themselves together [Fol. 44a, col. 1] to Adam, and he gave names to them as they bowed their heads before him. And at the second hour of Friday the Jews gathered themselves together against Christ, and they gnashed their teeth at Him, even as the blessed David said, "Many bulls have gathered together round about me, bulls of Bashan have beset me round" (Ps. xxii. 12).

At the THIRD HOUR of Friday a crown of glory was placed on the head of Adam, and at the third hour of Friday the crown of thorns was placed on the head of Christ.

THREE HOURS was Adam in Paradise and shining with splendour, and three hours was Christ in the Judgment Hall being beaten by creatures that had been fashioned out of dust.

At the SIXTH HOUR Eve went up to the tree of the transgression of the commandment, and at the sixth hour Christ ascended the Cross, the Tree of Life.

At the SIXTH HOUR Eve gave unto Adam the fruit of the gall of death [Fol. 44a, col. 2], and at the sixth hour the crowd of iniquity gave unto Christ vinegar and gall.

For THREE HOURS Adam remained under the Tree naked, and for three hours was Christ naked on the wood of the Cross. And from the right side of Adam went forth Eve, the mother of mortal offspring, and from the right side of Christ went forth baptism, the mother of immortal offspring.

On Friday Adam and Eve sinned, and on Friday their sin was remitted.

On Friday Adam and Eve died, and on Friday they came alive.

On Friday Death reigned over them, and on Friday they were freed from his dominion.

On Friday Adam and Eve went forth from Paradise, and on Friday our Lord went into the grave.

On Friday Adam and Eve became naked, and on Friday Christ stripped [Fol. 44b, col. 1] Himself naked and clothed them.

On Friday Satan stripped Adam and Eve naked, and on Friday Christ stripped naked Satan and all his hosts, and put them to shame openly.

On Friday the door of Paradise was shut and Adam went forth, and on Friday it was opened and a robber went in.

On Friday the two-edged sword was given to the Cherub, and on Friday Christ smote with the spear, and brake the two-edged sword.

On Friday kingdom, and priesthood, and prophecy were given unto Adam, and on Friday priesthood, and kingdom, and prophecy were taken from the Jews.

At the NINTH HOUR Adam went down into the lowest depth of the earth from the height of Paradise, and at the ninth hour Christ went down to the lowest depths of the earth, to those who lay [Fol. 44b, col. 2] in the dust, from the height of the Cross.

Know also that Christ was like unto Adam in everything, even as it is written. In that very place where Melchisedek ministered as a priest, and where Abraham offered up his son Isaac as an offering, the wood of the Cross was set up, and that self-same place is the centre of the earth, and there the Four Quarters of the earth meet each other. For when God made the earth His mighty power was running before it, and the earth was running after it, and the power of God stood still and became motionless in Golgotha; and that same place formeth the boundary of the earth. When Shem took up the body of Adam, that same place, which is the door of the earth, opened itself. And when Shem and Melchisedek had deposited the body of Adam in the centre of the earth the Four Quarters [Fol. 45a, col. 1] of the earth closed in about it, and embraced Adam, and straightway that opening was closed firmly, and all the children of Adam were not able to open it. And when the Cross of Christ, the Redeemer of Adam and his sons, was set up upon it, the door of that place was opened in the face of Adam. And when the Wood (i.e. the Cross) was fixed upon it, and Christ was smitten with the spear, and blood and water flowed down from His side, they ran down into the mouth of Adam, and they became a baptism to him, and he was baptized.

Now when the Jews crucified Christ on the Wood, they divided His garments among them beneath the Cross, even as it is written. His tunic was of purple, which is the raiment of royalty; and when they stripped Him of the raiment of royalty Pilate would not permit the Jews [Fol. 45a, col. 2] to array Him in ordinary apparel, but only in the actual raiment of royalty, either purple or scarlet. By both of these it might be known that He was a king. For it is impossible for any other man to wear purple; only a king can do this. And one of the Evangelists hath said, "The soldiers put on Him a purple robe" (Mark xv. 17; John xix. 2, 5), and this is a true word and is highly credible; and another Evangelist uses the word "scarlet "(Matt. xxvii. 28), and he proclaimed what was true. The scarlet garment indicateth to us blood, and the purple garment water; for the scarlet one was like unto blood, and the purple one was like unto water. The scarlet garment proclaimeth the joyful and immortal nature of man, and the purple one the sad and mortal nature of man. Understand, therefore, O our brother [Fol. 45b, col. 1] Nemesius, that scarlet proclaimeth life.

Now the spies said prophetically to Rahab, the harlot, "thou shalt tie a thread of scarlet to the window" (Joshua ii. 18) when they descended having been [well] entreated by her. And through her they prefigured a certain matter, for the window [symbolized] the side of our Lord Christ, and the thread of scarlet His precious blood which produced life.

And they (i.e. the Jews) wove a crown of spikes of thorn bushes, and set it upon His head. And they arrayed Him in royal apparel, not knowing what they were doing. And they bowed the knee, and made obeisance unto Him, and they spake with their mouths, without being compelled to do so, saying, "Hail to Thee, King of the Jews." Observe ye, O my brethren, that not even in His death did He lack the [sign of] royalty. And when the Jews and the soldiers who were the servants of Herod and Pilate were struggling together to rend the tunic of Christ [Fol. 45b, col. 2], to divide it among them, they did so because they all eagerly desired the beauty of the sight thereof. And the centurion also who watched the Cross himself testified before all the crowd, saying, "Verily, this man is the Son of God." And this centurion said unto them, "The orders which have been given to me do not permit me to rend the apparel of royalty, but cast lots for it [and we shall see] to whom it will come"; and when the Jews and the soldiers of the king had cast lots, the lot fell upon one of the soldiers of Pilate. Now the tunic of our Lord had no seam, but had been woven whole in one piece. And whensoever there was a lack of rain in the place where it had been deposited and taken care of, the people used to bring out the tunic, and as soon as they lifted it up [Fol. 46a, col. 1] towards heaven an abundance of rain fell. And also, whensoever the soldier who had received it lacked rain for his crop, he brought out the tunic, and it worked this miracle. Now the tunic was taken away by force from the man who got it by Pilate, who sent it to the Emperor Tiberius. To us this tunic indicateth the Orthodox Faith, which all the nations [joined] together are unable to cleave.

Three valuable gifts, than which there is nothing more valuable, were given to the Jews in olden time, namely, royalty, priesthood, and prophecy: prophecy by the hand of Moses, priesthood by the hand of Aaron, and royalty by the hand of David. These three gifts which the generations and families of the children of Israel had enjoyed for [many] years were taken from them in one day; and they were stripped of all three of them, and became aliens to them, that is to say, prophecy by the Cross, priesthood by the rending of the tunic [of Christ], and royalty by the crown of thorns. Moreover, that spirit of compassion (or propitiation) which had dwelt in the Temple, in the Holy of Holies, forsook them and departed. And the curtain (or veil) of the sanctuary was cleft in twain. And the Passover fled from them, for they never celebrated another Passover in it. And know, O my brethren, that when Pilate pressed them to go into the Judgment Hall, they said unto him, "We are unable to go into the Prætorium, because up to now we have not eaten the Passover."

And when the sentence of death had been passed on our Lord by Pilate, they (the Jews) made haste and went into the sanctuary [Fol. 46b, col. 1] and brought out from thence the carrying poles of the Ark of the Covenant, and out of them they made the Cross of Christ. Verily it was meet that these pieces of wood which used to carry the Covenant should also carry the Lord of the Covenant. The Cross of Christ was formed of two pieces of wood which were of the same height, and depth, and length, and breadth. And Paul the Apostle laboured exceedingly that the Gentiles might know what was the might of the Cross, which embraced the height, and depth, and length, and breadth of the earth. And when they raised up Christ, the Lamp of Light of all the earth, and set Him upon the candlestick of the Cross, the light of the sun became dark, and was extinguished, and a covering of darkness was spread over the whole earth. Three nails were driven into the body of our Redeemer, two through His hands, and one through both His feet. And there were two thieves [with Him], one on His right hand and one on His left hand.

And they handed out to Him vinegar and gall in a sponge. By the vinegar which they gave unto Him it was made known concerning them that their will was changed from what it had been formerly, and that they had turned themselves from integrity to wickedness, and by the gall was made known the bitterness of the accursed serpent which was in them. And they showed that they also had belonged to that good vineyard from which prophets, and kings, and priests, and they themselves had drunk; but because they had become wicked heirs, who would not labour in the vineyard of my beloved, they produced husks instead of grapes, and the wine which they pressed out therefrom was sour. And having crucified the Heir on the Wood, they mixed some of the impurity of their wickedness with their sour wine [Fol. 47a, col. 1], and gave Him to drink of the wine from the vineyard of the Gentiles; but He would not drink [saying], "Give me of that vine which My Father brought out of Egypt." For Christ knew that the prophecy of Moses which had been prophesied concerning them had been fulfilled in them; for Moses said, "Your grapes are grapes of gall, your clusters are bitter. Your poison is the poison of the serpent, and their head is that of a malignant viper. These are the things which ye render unto the Lord" (Deut. xxxii. 32, 33).

Observe, O my brother Nemesius, that the blessed Moses with the eye of the Spirit foresaw the things which they were going to do to Christ [and said], "These are the things which ye render to the Lord." The congregation of the crucifiers was a decayed vine, its daughters were bitter grapes, and its sons were clusters of gall. Their head was Caiaphas, the malignant viper, and they were all evil serpents, and all of them were filled with [Fol. 47a, col. 2] the venom of Satan, who is the Evil Serpent. Instead of the water of the rock which had been given them to drink in the wilderness, they gave Him vinegar to drink, and instead of manna, the gall of the quail. They did not give Him a cup to drink from, but a sponge, so that they might show that the blessing of their fathers had been swept away from them. Now this is evident from what follows: When a vessel is empty and there is no wine in it, they wash and wipe it with a sponge. Even so did the Jews do when they crucified Christ, [for] with a sponge they wiped away and removed from themselves royalty, and priesthood, and prophecy, and the religion of Christ, and gave them to Christ, and the vessels of their bodies washed and empty remained only.

And the Law and the Prophets having been fulfilled, and Adam having been sent and seen the fountain of living water which was poured out from above for his redemption [Fol. 47b, col. 1], then was Christ smitten with the spear, and blood and water flowed down from His side; but they were not mingled with each other. For what reason did the blood come forth before the water? For two reasons: First, that through the blood life might be given unto Adam, and then, after life and resurrection, the water for his baptism. Secondly, that through the blood He might show that He was immortal, and through the water He might show that He was mortal, and a bearer of sufferings. The blood and the water ran down into the mouth of Adam, and Adam was redeemed, and put on a garment of glory. And Christ wrote the edict of His return with the blood of His own Person, and despatched it by the thief.

And when an end had been made of everything, the writ of repudiation of the congregation was written, and the congregation became a thing cast aside, and it was stripped of its glorious raiment, even as in times of old [Fol. 47b, col. 2] David had, through the Holy Spirit, said and prophesied, saying, "Even unto the horns of the altar" (Ps. cxviii. 22 ?)--to this pass were the festivals of the Jews brought. "Unto the horns of the altar" [means] to the crucifixion of Christ, that is to say:

The Genealogy of Christ

From Adam to Seth; from Seth to Enos; from Enos to Cainan; from Cainan to Mahalâlâêl; from Mahalâlâêl to Jared; from Jared to Enoch; from Enoch to Methuselah; from Methuselah to Lamech; from Lamech to Noah; from Noah to Shem; from Shem to Arphaxad; from Arphaxad to Salah; from Salah to Eber; from Eber to Peleg; from Peleg to Reu; from Reu to Serug; from Serug to Nahor; from Nahor to Terah; from Terah to Abraham; from Abraham to Isaac; from Isaac to Jacob; from Jacob [Fol. 48a, col. 1] to Judah; from Judah to Pharez; from Pharez to Hesron; from Hesron to Aram; from Aram to Amminadab; from Amminadab to Nahasson; from Nahasson to Salmon; from Salmon to Boaz; from Boaz to Obed; from Obed to Jesse; from Jesse to David; from David to Solomon; from Solomon to Rehoboam; from Rehoboam to Abijah; from Abijah to Ara; from Ara to Jehoshaphat; from Jeshoshaphat to Joram; from Joram to Ahaziah; from Ahaziah to Joash; from Joash to Amaziah; from Amaziah to Uzziah; from Uzziah to Jotham; from Jotham to Ahaz; from Ahaz to Hezekiah; from Hezekiah to Manasseh; from Manasseh to Ammon; from Ammon to Josiah; from Josiah to Jehoahaz; from Jehoahaz to Jehoiakim; from Jehoiakim to Jehoiachin; from Jehoiachin to Salathiel; from Salathiel [Fol. 48a, col. 2] to Zerubbabel; from Zerubbabel to Abiud; from Abiud to Eliakim; from Eliakim to Azor; from Azor to Zadok; from Zadok to Achin; from Achin to Eliud; from Eliud to Eleazar; from Eleazar to Mathan; from Mathan to Jacob and Yônâkhîr; from Yônâkhîr to Mary; from Mary to the manger; from the manger to circumcision; from the circumcision to the Temple; from the Temple to Egypt; from Egypt to Galilee; from Galilee to Jerusalem; from Jerusalem to the Jordan; from the Jordan to the desert; from the desert to Judah; from Judah to the preaching; from the preaching to the Upper Chamber; from the Upper Chamber to the Passover; from the Passover to the Judgment Hall; from the Judgment Hall to the Cross; from the Cross to the grave; from the grave to the Upper Chamber; from the Upper Chamber to heaven; and from heaven to the throne [Fol. 48b, col. 1]. He sitteth on the right hand of His Father.

The end of the two and sixty weeks

Observe, O our brother Nemesius, how the generations and families have succeeded each other; from Adam to the Jews, and the Jews also from one [generation] to another until the Cross of Christ. From that time and onwards the festivals of the Jews have ceased, even as the blessed David saith concerning them: "Bind our festivals with chains even to the horns of the altar" (Ps. cxviii. 27). The chains are the families which are linked each to the other, and the altar is the Cross of Christ. The festivals of the Jews succeeded each other until the Cross of Christ, in priesthood, and royalty, and prophecy, and Passover; but from the Cross of Christ up to the present they all have ceased, even as I have said [Fol. 48b, col. 2]. The Jews have no longer among them a king, or a priest, or a prophet, or a Passover, even as Daniel prophesied concerning them, saying, "After two and sixty weeks Christ shall be slain, and the city of holiness shall be laid waste until the completion of things decreed" (Dan. ix. 26). That is to say, for ever and ever.

Christ's body is embalmed and laid in the tomb made for Joshua, the son of Nôn

And when the end of all the Law and the Prophets had come, and Christ was hanging on the Cross, Joseph, the brother of Nicodemus and Cleophas, went in to Pilate--now he was the bearer of the seal-ring of Pilate, and was a councillor, and had free intercourse with him--and asked for the body of our Redeemer; and Pilate commanded that it should be given to him. And when Joseph had taken His body, straightway Pilate commanded that [Fol. 49a, col. 1] the garden also in which the grave was situated should be given to him; it belonged to Joseph, and it had been given unto him as an inheritance by Phinehas, the Levite, the son of Joseph's uncle. Now Joseph was from Jerusalem, but he had been made a councillor in Râmthâ, and all the letters which had been written during the whole period of Pilate's administration had been sealed with the seal which Joseph carried. And when Joseph had taken down the body of our Lord from the Cross, the Jews ran and took the Cross, and brought it into the Temple, because [the pieces of wood thereof] were the bearing poles of the Ark of the Covenant. And Nicodemos also embalmed the body of our Lord [and swathed it] in clean, new linen swathings, and Joseph made it ready for the grave and buried it in a new tomb which had been made for Joshua, the son of Nôn, to be buried in. And because he saw with the eye of the Spirit [Fol. 49a, col. 2], and the way of the Dispensation of Christ had appeared to him, he took the stone which had travelled about with the children of Israel in the desert and placed it at the door of the tomb, and therefore he was not buried in it. And when Joseph, and Nicodemus, and Cleophas had buried Christ, they laid that stone before the door of the building of the tomb. And the high priests, and men of the house of Pilate, went out and set seals on the grave and on the stone.

The Cross of Christ

And now, my brother Nemesius, be amazed and give praise to God that all the straps (or, ligatures) of the . . . . . . of Christ were joined together on the bearing poles of the Ark of the service of God and the covering of the sanctuary of propitiation. This was what God commanded Moses: to make a breast-plate of judgment (Exod. xxviii. 15) and of peace; of judgment for the Jews who crucified Him [Fol. 49b, col. 1], and of peace for the Gentiles who have believed in him. His Cross was made of the wood of the Sanctuary, His grave was a new one, which had been made for the death of Joshua, the son of Nôn, and the stone (or rock), which is Christ, had when in the desert given water to six hundred thousand people, and now it became an altar and gave life to all the Gentiles. And the saying of the Apostle, "that rock was Christ" (I Cor. x. 4) is true and well worthy of belief. Joseph was a councillor in Râmthâ, Nicodemus was a teacher of the Law in Jerusalem, and Cleophas was the recorder of the Hebrews in 'Amâôs. Nicodemus prepared everything which was required for the Passover in the Upper Chamber; and Joseph made Him ready for burial and buried Him in his own inheritance, and Cleophas received Him into his house. And when [Fol. 49b, col. 2] He had risen from the dead these men became to Him true and faithful brethren.

The trilingual inscription above the Cross

And when Joseph brought Him down from the Cross, he took away that inscription which was spread out above His head, that is to say, over the head of the Cross of Christ, because it had been written by Pilate in Greek, and Latin, and Hebrew. And why did Pilate write in it no word of the Syrians? Because the Syrians participated in no way whatsoever in the [shedding of the] blood of Christ. And Pilate, a wise man and a lover of the truth, did not wish to write a lie as wicked judges do, but he did according to what is written in the Law of Moses. Pilate wrote in the inscription [the names of the languages of] those who condemned the innocent in the order in which the slayers of Christ laid their hands upon him, and he hung the writing above Him. Herod was a Greek, Caiaphas was [Fol. 50a, col. 1] a Hebrew, and Pilate a Roman. Now the Syrians had no part in the murder of Christ, and to this testifieth Abhgar, king of Edessa, who wished to take Jerusalem and destroy it because the Jews crucified Christ. [See Cureton, Doctrine of Addai, ed. Phillips, page 30; Cureton, Ancient Syrian Documents, page 107; and Wright, Journal of Sacred Literature, No. XX, New Series, January, 1865.

The Harrowing of Hell

Now the descent of Sheol was not in vain, for it was the cause of manifold benefits to our race. He dismissed Death from his domination. He preached the resurrection to those who were lying in the dust, and He pardoned those who had sinned against the Law. He laid waste Sheol, and slew sin. He put Satan to shame, and made the devils sad, and He abrogated sacrifices and offerings and made an apology for Adam, and abolished the festivals of the Jews.

NOTE.--According to the Coptic Book of the Resurrection, which is attributed to Bartholomew the Apostle, Christ broke down the doors of hell, and smashed the bolts, and destroyed the doorposts and frames. He overthrew the blazing furnaces of brass, and extinguished their fires, and, sweeping everything out of hell, He left it like a desert. He fettered the "Shameless One," and bound the ministers of Satan, and tied up a devil called Melkhir with a chain. See British Museum MS. Oriental No. 6804, and Budge, Coptic Apocrypha, page 184.

The Resurrection of Christ

And having risen from the grave on the third day, Christ appeared to Kîpâ (Peter) and John.

And whilst [Fol. 50a, col. 2] Christ was in the grave, and the watchmen were sitting round about it, Simon Peter conceived the design of giving the watchmen wine to drink so that they might become drunk and fall asleep, when he intended to rise up and open the tomb, and take out the body of Christ without breaking the seals on the tomb, so that the Jews might not say, "Assuredly His disciples stole Him away." And whilst the watchmen were eating and drinking, Christ rose up and showed Himself to Kîpâ (Peter), for He had indeed risen. And Peter believed that He was truly

Christ, the Lord of the heavens and the earth, and did not approach the tomb. And afterwards Christ also appeared to the watchmen openly, and He went to His disciples in the Upper Chamber, and Thomas felt Him. And He appeared to His disciples on the sea shore. Now, though Simon Peter denied Him thrice before the Jews, he acknowledged Him thrice [Fol. 50b, col. 1] before the disciples. And Christ delivered to him and committed to his hands all His flock, saying, before His disciples, "Feed thou for Me My sheep and lambs and ewes," that is to say, men, women and children. And forty days after His Resurrection He bestowed upon the Apostles the laying on of hands of the priesthood, and He went up to heaven, and sat down on the right hand of His Father.

Then the Apostles gathered themselves together and went up into the Upper Chamber with Mary, the Holy Virgin, and Simon Peter baptized Mary, and John, the virgin, received her [into his house]. And they decreed a fast until they had received the Spirit, the Paraclete, at Pentecost, they all being gathered together. And tongues (i.e. languages) were distributed among them, so that each of them might go and teach that nation in the tongue which he had received, so that there might never be strife among them. [Fol. 50b, col. 2].

TESTAMENTUM ADAMI

THE HOURS OF THE DAY

ND, moreover, understand thou concerning the hours of the day and of the night, and how it is seemly that ye should make supplication to God, and to pray to Him at each of His seasons. For my Creator taught me all this, and He told me the names of all the wild animals and beasts, and of the birds of heaven, and then God made me to understand the number of the hours of the day and of the night, and He told me how the angels praise God. Understand, then, O my son, that at the first hour of the day the prayer of my children ascendeth to God. And at the second hour the prayer and petition of the angels take place. At the third hour the birds of the heavens praise Him. And at the fourth hour the spiritual beings worship Him. And at the fifth hour all the wild beasts and animals salute Him. At the sixth hour the petition of the Kîrûbêl (Cherubim) taketh place. And at the seventh hour all the angels enter the presence of God, and go forth therefrom, for at this hour the prayer of every living thing ascendeth to God. At the eighth hour the shining denizens of heaven praise Him. And at the ninth hour the angels of God who stand before the throne of the Most High do homage unto Him. And at the tenth hour the Holy Spirit overshadoweth the waters, and the devils flee away and remove themselves from the waters. And if the Holy Spirit did not overshadow the waters at this hour every day, no one could drink of the waters, [for if he did] his flesh (i.e. body) would be destroyed by the evil devils. And if the priest taketh water at this hour and mixeth with it holy oil, and anointeth the sick and those who are possessed of foul spirits with the mixture, they shall be healed of their sickness. And at the eleventh hour the glorifyings of the righteous take place. And at the twelfth hour God, the Most High, receiveth the prayers and petitions of the children of men.

THE HOURS OF THE NIGHT

And at the first hour of the night the devils render thanks and praise to God Most High, and there is in them no evil and no harm for anyone until they have finished their service of homage. And at the second hour of the night the fish and every creature that is in the waters praise God, and the wild beasts and the whales. And at the third hour the fire praiseth Him--now it is in the lowest depth, and in that hour no one can address Him (?). And at the fourth hour the Sûrâfêl (Seraphim) proclaim Him Holy. And at the fifth hour the waters which are above the heavens praise Him. Now long ago I sat and listened to the angels at this hour, and [marvelled] how they cried out; [their cry] was like the noise of a mighty wheel, and they cried out like the waves of the sea with the voice of praise to God. And at the sixth hour the clouds praised God in fear and trembling. And at the seventh hour the earth was hushed in silence and every creature that was upon it, and the waters slumbered. And if at this hour the priest taketh some water and mixeth holy oil with it, and he anointeth therewith the sick and those who cannot sleep at night because of [their] pain, those who are sick will be healed, and those who are wakeful will fall asleep. At the eighth hour the earth maketh to grow grass and green herbs, and maketh the trees to put forth leaves and fruit. And at the ninth hour the angels perform their service of homage to God, and the prayer of the children of men cometh into the presence of God the Most High. And at the tenth hour the gates of heaven are opened, and God heareth the prayer of the children of the believers, and the petition which they ask from God is granted unto them; And at the sound of the wings of the Seraphim at that time the cocks crow and praise God. And at the eleventh hour there is joy and gladness on all the earth, for the sun entereth into the Garden (i.e. Paradise), and his light riseth in all the ends of the world, and illumineth every created thing. And at the twelfth hour it is befitting for my children to stand up before God, and pay homage to Him, for at this hour there resteth a great silence on all the heavenly beings.

ADAM FORETELLS THE COMING OF CHRIST

Now therefore know thou all this, and hearken unto my word, and understand that the Word of God, the Most High, shall come down upon the earth, even as He told me at the moment when He thrust me out from the Garden (Paradise). For He told me that His Word in later days should become man from a woman who was a virgin whose name was Mary, and should hide in her, and put on flesh, and be born like a man with great power, and operative skill and knowledge. No one shall know Him except Himself and him to whom He manifested [Himself]. And God said that He should go about with people on the earth, and grow in days and years, and should perform signs and wonders openly, and should walk upon the sea as upon dry land, and should rebuke the sea and the winds openly, and they should be subject unto Him, and that He should cry out to the waves of the sea and they should make answer to Him speedily. And that He should make the blind to see, and the lepers to be cleansed, and the deaf to hear, and the dumb to talk, and should raise up the paralytics, and make the lame to walk, and should turn many from error to the knowledge of God, and should drive out the devils from men.

And besides [these things] God spake unto me, saying, "Be not sorrowful, O Adam, for thou didst wish to become a god and didst transgress my command. Behold, I will stablish thee, not at this present, but after a few days." And again He spake unto me, saying, "I am God Who made thee to go forth from the Garden of Joy into the earth, which shall shoot forth thorns and brambles, and thou shalt dwell therein. Bend thy back, and make thy knees to totter in old age, and I will make thy flesh food for the worms. And after five days and half a day[5] I will have compassion upon thee, and shew thee mercy in the abundance of my compassion and my mercy. And I will come down into thy house, and I will dwell in thy flesh, and for thy sake I will be pleased to be born like an [ordinary] child. And for thy sake I will be pleased to walk in the market place. And for thy sake I will be pleased to fast forty days. And for thy sake I will be pleased to accept baptism. And for thy sake I will be pleased to endure suffering. And for thy sake I will be pleased to hang on the wood of the Cross. All these things [will I do] for thy sake, O Adam."

To Him be praise, and majesty, and dominion, and glory, and worship, and hymns, with His Father and the Holy Spirit from this time forward and for ever and ever. Amen.

Furthermore, thou must know, O my son, Seth, behold a Flood shall come and shall wash the whole earth because of the children of Kâyal (Cain), the murderer, who slew his brother through jealousy, because of his sister Lûd. And after the Flood and many weeks the latter days shall come, and everything shall be completed, and his time shall come and fire shall consume everything which is found before God, and the earth shall be sanctified, and the Lord of Lords shall walk about on it."

And Seth wrote down this Commandment, and sealed it with his seal, and with the seal of his father Adam, which he took with him from the Garden (Paradise), and with the seal of Eve his mother.

SUPPLEMENTARY TRANSLATIONS FROM THE "BOOK OF THE BEE"

THE ASSUMPTION OF THE VIRGIN. OUR LORD'S APPEARANCES AFTER THE RESURRECTION. THE LAST SUPPER. THE NAMES OF THE APOSTLES AND DISCIPLES. CHRONOLOGY. GOG AND MAGOG. ANTI-CHRIST. THE GREEK TRANSLATION OF THE HEBREW BIBLE

THE extracts quoted in the preceding pages show how largely Solomon, Bishop of Al-Basrah, borrowed from the "Cave of Treasures" when compiling his work, "The Book of the Bee," especially when he was dealing with the history of the early Patriarchs. But he did not bring his book to a close with the narrative of the Crucifixion, for his aim was to describe briefly the progress of Christianity after the death of Christ; and in doing this he collected and set down in writing a considerable amount of information regarding the Apostles and disciples, and their lives and deaths, and a number of facts and legends which he accepted and wished the Nestorians in his diocese especially to believe. In fact, the "Book of the Bee," though written by a Nestorian bishop, may be regarded as a supplement or continuation of the "Cave of Treasures," which, according to ancient tradition, was written by a Jacobite bishop. Both works are included in the collection of texts which the learned priest Hômô copied in the British Museum MS. Add. 25875, and both were so highly esteemed that copies of them were made for the library of the church of the Virgin Mary in `Amedîa. The following summary is based on my translation of the Syriac text published at Oxford in 1886.

THE DEATH AND ASSUMPTION OF THE VIRGIN MARY

Mary lived twelve years after our Lord's Ascension; the sum of the years which she lived in the world was fifty-eight years, but others say sixty-one years. She was not buried on earth, but the angels carried her to Paradise, and angels bore her bier. On the other hand, we read in the History of the Virgin, "And the blessed Mary departed this life in the year of Alexander, 394 (i.e. A.D. 82-83). At the Annunciation she was thirty years old, and she lived also the thirty-three years of the Dispensation; and after the

Crucifixion she lived fifty-eight years. The years which she lived were one hundred and twenty-one." In the same book we have: "And Mary remained in Jerusalem, and grieved because of her separation from our Lord Jesus Christ, and the absence of the apostles from her. And she prayed and cast frankincense into the fire, and lifted up her eyes and spread out her hands to heaven, and said, 'O Christ, the Son of the living God, hearken unto the voice of Thy handmaiden, and send unto me Thy friend John the Young with his fellow-apostles, that I may see them and be comforted by the sight of them before the day of my death; and I will praise and adore Thy goodness.'" And straightway it was revealed by the Holy Spirit to each one of the apostles, in whatever country he was in, that the blessed Mary was about to depart from this world into the never-ending life. And the Spirit summoned them, along with those of them who were dead, to be gathered together at daybreak to the blessed Mary for her to see them: and each one of them came to her from his own land at dawn by the agency of the Holy Spirit, and they saluted Mary and each other, and adored her. Thomas was in India, and an angel took him up and brought him. And he found the angels carrying her bier through the air; and they brought it nigh to Thomas, and he also prayed and was blessed by her.

OUR LORD'S APPEARANCES AFTER HIS RESURRECTION

He appeared ten times: 1. To Mary Magdalene (John xx. 11, 18). 2. To the women at the grave (Matt. xxviii. 9, 10). 3. To Cleophas (Luke xxiv. 18). 4. To Simon Peter (Luke xxiv. 34). 5. To all the disciples except Thomas (Luke xxiv. 36-49; John xx. 19-23). 6. To the disciples, Thomas being with them (John xx. 24-29). 7. On the Mount (Matt. xxviii. 16-20). 8. On the Sea of Tiberias (John xxi. 1-24). 9. At His Ascension (Mark xvi. 19; Luke xxiv. 50-53). 10. To the Five Hundred at once (I Cor. xv. 6). After His Ascension he appeared to Paul (Acts ix. 3-9; I Cor. xv. 3), and to Stephen (Acts vii. 55-60).

THE LAST SUPPER

Some men have a tradition that when our Lord broke His body in the Upper Chamber, John, the son of Zebedee, hid a part of his portion until our Lord rose from the dead. When Thomas put his finger near to our Lord's side, and it rested on the mark of the spear, the disciples saw the blood. And John took that piece of consecrated bread, and wiped up that blood with it; and the Easterns Mâr Addai and Mâr Mârî took that piece, and sanctified this unleavened bread which has been handed down among us. Others say that when John took that piece of consecrated bread in his hand, it burst into flame, and burnt in the palm of his hand, and the palm of his hand sweated, and he took that sweat and hid it for the sign of the Cross of baptism.

THE APOSTLES

The Apostles were Twelve and Seventy; their names are:--

SIMON, the chief of the Apostles, was from Bethsaida, of the tribe of Naphtali. He preached for one year in Antioch, where the disciples were [first] called Christians, and he built there the first church, in the house of Cassianus, whose son he restored to life. He lived in Rome twenty-seven years. He was crucified, head downwards, by Nero, in the 376th year of the Greeks (65-64 B.C.).

ANDREW, his brother, preached in Scythia, Nicomedia, and Achaia. He died in Byzantium and was buried in the church which he built there.

JOHN, the son of Zabhdai (Zebedee), was from Bethsaida, of the tribe of Zebulon. He preached in Ephesus, was exiled to Patmos, and then returned to Ephesus, where he built a church. Three of his disciples went with him:-- IGNATIUS, later bishop of Antioch, who was thrown to the beasts in Rome; POLYCARP, later bishop of Smyrna who was burnt to death; and JOHN, who succeeded him as bishop. John, the son of Zebedee, was buried by John, his disciple, at Ephesus, and his grave is unknown. John, his disciple, was also buried at Ephesus. He wrote the Revelation, and said that all he had written in that book he had received from John the Evangelist.

JAMES, the brother of John, preached in Bethsaida and built a church there. Herod Agrippa slew him with the sword in the year following the Ascension of our Lord. He was buried at Âkâr, a city of Marmârîkâ.

PHILIP, from Bethsaida, was of the tribe of Asher. He preached in Phrygia, Pamphylia and Pisidia; he died in Pisidia, and was buried in the church which he built there. He lived as an apostle 27 years.

THOMAS, from Jerusalem, was of the tribe of Judah. He taught the Parthians, Medes and Indians; he baptized the daughter of the Indian king, who had him speared to death. Habbân the merchant brought his body to Edessa and buried it there. Some say he was buried in Mahlûph in India.

MATTHEW, from Nazareth, was of the tribe of Issachar. He preached in Palestine, Tyre and Sidon, and went as far as Gabbûlâ (i.e. al-Jabbâl, a town in Coelesyria). He died, and was buried in Antioch.

BARTHOLOMEW, from Endor, was of the tribe of Issachar. He preached in Armenia, Ardeshîr, Ketarbôl, Radbîn and Prûharmân. He first went to Golthon in Armenia, came back to Artaschu, and then went on to Her, Zarevant and Urbianos. He lived as an apostle for 30 years, and then Hûrstî (Rhûstnî or Hêrôstmî), king of Armenia, crucified him in Urbianos. He was buried in the church which he had built in Armenia. The king of Armenia in the time of Bartholomew was called Sanadrog (Sanatruk).

JUDE, the son of James, surnamed THADDAEUS (TADDAI), who is also LEBBAEUS (Lebbai), from Jerusalem, was of the tribe of Judah. He preached in Laodicea, and in Antaradus and Arwâd (Ruwâd). He was stoned in Arwâd, and died and was buried there.

SIMON ZELÔTES, from Galilee, was of the tribe of Ephraim. He preached in Shêmêshât (Samosata), Pârîn (Perrhê), Zeugma, Hâlâb (Aleppo), Mabbôg (Manbig), and Kenneshrîn (Kinnesrîn). He built a church in Kyrrhos, and died and was buried there.

JAMES, the son of Alphaeus (Halphai), was from the Jordan, and of the tribe of Manasseh. He preached in Tadmor (Palmyra), Kirkêsion (Kîrkîsîyâ), and Callinicos (ar-Rakkah), and came to Bâtnân of Serûg (Sarug), where he built a church, and died and was buried there.

JUDAS ISCARIOT, the Betrayer, from Sekharyût, was of the tribe of Gad or Dan. MATTHIAS, of the tribe of Reuben, came in his stead. He preached in Hellas and in Sicily, where he built a church, and died, and was buried in it.

JAMES, the brother of our Lord, was cast down from a pinnacle of the Temple whilst preaching in Jerusalem; then a fuller of cloth smashed in his skull with a club, and afterwards they stoned him.

JOHN THE BAPTIST was of the tribe of Levi. Herod the tetrarch slew him, and his body was buried in Sebastia.

ANANIAS (HANANYÂ), John's disciple, taught in Damascus and Arbîl. Pôl, the general of Aretas (Aristus) slew him, and he was buried in his church at Arbil.

PAUL, of Tarsus, was a Pharisee and of the tribe of Ephraim (or, Benjamin ?). He went to Peter at Rome, and Nero ordered them to be slain. On their way to the place of slaughter they gave the laying on of hands of the priesthood to their disciples, Peter to Mark, and Paul to Luke. Peter was crucified and Paul was beheaded, and Mark and Luke brought their bodies into the city. But Paul's head could not be found. At length a shepherd found it, and he laid it by his sheep-fold. At night a fire blazed over it, and the shepherd went and told bishop Xystus and the clergy, and when they saw the head they recognized it as Paul's head. They laid the head at the feet of Paul's body, and, having prayed the whole night, the head was found to have joined itself to the body. From his call to the end of his life was 35 years; he travelled for 31 years, and he was in prison at Caesarea for two years, and for two years in Rome. He was martyred in the thirty-sixth year after the Passion of our Lord, and was buried in the royal catacombs in Rome.

LUKE, the physician and Evangelist, was a disciple of Lazarus, and was baptized by Philip in the city of Beroea. He was beheaded by Hôros, the governor of Alexandria under Tiberius, whilst preaching there; he was buried in that city.

MARK the Evangelist preached in Rome, and died and was buried there. He was either the son of Simon Peter's wife or the son of Simon; and Rhoda was his sister. He was first called John, but the Apostles changed his name to Mark.

ADDAI, from Paneas, preached in Edessa and Mesopotamia in the days of Abhgar the king; he built a church in Edessa. Herod, son of Abhgar, slew him in the fortress of Aggêl, or Engîl, north of Amid. He was buried either in Edessa or Rome.

AGGAI, the disciple of Addai, was a silk weaver; because he refused to give up his preaching, Herod, son of Abhgar, broke his legs with a club and he killed him.

THADDAEUS was slain by Herod, son of Abhgar, and was buried in Edessa.

ZACCHAEUS (Zaccai), the publican, was slain whilst preaching in Mount Hôrôn.

SIMON, the leper, taught in Ramah, and the Jews slew him there.

JOSEPH, the Senator, taught in Galilee and Decapolis, and was buried in Ramah.

NICODEMUS, the Pharisee, the friend of our Lord, died in Jerusalem, and was buried there. Some say that he was buried by his brother Gamaliel in Kephar Gamlâ.

NATHANIEL was stoned whilst preaching in Mount Hôrôn (or, Mount Hebron), and died.

SIMON, the Cyrenian, was slain in the island of Chios.

SIMON, son of Cleopas, was bishop of Jerusalem. At the age of one hundred years he was crucified by Irenaeus (or, Hereôs?), the chiliarch.

STEPHEN was stoned to death in Jerusalem, and was buried in Kephar Gamlâ.

MARK (surnamed John) taught at Nyssa and Nazianzus; he built a church at the latter place, and died and was buried there.

GEPHAS (Gal. ii. 9; I Cor. i. 12) taught in Baalbec, Hims (Emesa), and Nathrôn (Batharûn); he died and was buried in Shîrâz (Shaizar ?).

BARNABAS, a native of Cyprus or a member of a family of Cyprians settled in Antioch, undertook two preaching missions in that Island, and then went and preached in Northern Italy and Kûrâ for some time. Later he returned to Cyprus, where, according to one tradition, he suffered martyrdom. The various accounts of his life and preaching are described by Lipsius in his Apostelgeschichte (Bd. ii. Heft 2, pp. 276-320).

TITUS taught in Crete, and died and was buried there.

SOSTHENES taught in Pontus and Asia, and was cast into the sea by Nonnus, the prefect.

CRISCUS (CRESCENS) taught in Dalmatia; he died of hunger in Alexandria.

JUSTUS taught in Tiberias and Caesarea, where he died and was buried.

ANDRONICUS taught in Illyricum, where he died and was buried.

RUFUS was slain whilst teaching in Zeugma.

PATROBAS taught in Chalcedon, and died there.

HERMAS, the shepherd, taught in Antioch and died there.

NARCISSUS taught in Hellas, and died there.

ASYNCRITUS went to Bêth-Hûzâyê (Ahwâz, Khûzistân), and died there.

ARISTOBULUS taught in Isauria, and died there.

ONESIMUS, the slave of Philemon, fled to Paul in Rome, where his legs were broken, and he died.

APOLLOS was burned to death by Sparacleus (?), governor of Gangra.

OLYMPAS, STACHYS and STEPHEN died in prison in Tarsus.

JUNIAS was slain in Samos.

THEOCRITUS died in Ilios.

MARTALUS (I) was slain by the Barbarians.

NIGER taught in Antioch, and died there.

LUCIUS was dragged behind a horse and died.

ALEXANDER was thrown into a pit in Heracleôpolis (Hierapolis ?) and died.

MILUS was drowned at Rhodes.

SILVANUS and HERÔDIÔN (Rhôdiôn) were slain at Accô.

SILAS taught at Sarapolis (Hierapolis ?), and died there.

TIMOTHY taught in Ephesus, and died there.

MANAEL was burned to death in Accô.

The EUNUCH of Candace was strangled on the island of Parparchia.

JASON and SOSIPATRUS were thrown to the beasts in Olmius.

DEMAS taught in Thessalonica, and died there.

OMIUS (HYMENAEUS) taught in Melitene, and died there.

THRASEUS was thrown into a fiery furnace at Laodicea.

BISTORIUS (ARISTARCHUS) taught in the island of Kâ, and died there.

ABRIOS and MÔTOS died in Ethiopia.

LEVI was slain in Paneas by Charmus.

NICETIANUS (NICETAS) was sawn in twain in Tiberias.

JOHN and THEODORUS were thrown to the beasts at Baalbec.

EUCHESTION (?) and SIMON were slain by Methalius in Byzantium.

EPHRAIM (APHREM) taught in Baishân, and died there.

JUSTUS was slain at Corinth.

JAMES taught in Nicomedia, and died there.

THE NAMES OF THE APOSTLES

The TWELVE (Matt. x. Mark iii. Luke vi. Acts i.).

1. Simon Peter.
2. Andrew, his brother.
3. James, the son of Zebedee.
4. John, his brother.
5. Philip.
6. Bartholomew.
7. Thomas.
8. Matthew.
9. James, the son of Alphaeus.
10. Labbaeus (Thaddaeus).
11. Simon the Canaanite.
12. Judas Iscariot (in whose stead came Matthias).

The SEVENTY.

1. James, the son of Joseph.
2. Simon, the son of Cleopas.
3. Cleopas, his father.
4-8. Joses; Simon; Judah; Barnabas; Manaeus (?).
9. Ananias, who baptized Paul.
10. Cephas, who preached at Antioch.
11. Joseph, the senator.
12. Nicodemus, the Archon.
13. Nathaniel, the chief scribe.
14. Justus (i.e. Joseph, called Barshabbâ).
15-17. Silas; Judah; John (Mark).
18. Mnason, who received Paul.
19. Manael, foster-brother of Herod.
20. Simon, called Niger.
21. Jason (see Acts xvii. 5-9).
22. Rufus (see Rom. xvi. 13).
23. Alexander.
24. Simon, the Cyrenian, their father.
25. Lucius, the Cyrenian.
26. Judah (mentioned in the Acts).
27. Judah, who is called Simon.
28. Eurion (Orion), the splay-footed.
29-32. Thorus; Thorisus; Zabdon; Zakron.

The following were chosen with Stephen:--

33. Philip, whose three (sic) daughters prophesied (see Acts xxi. 9).

34-36. Stephen; Prochorus; Nicanor.

37-39. Timon; Parmenas; Nicolaus (Acts vi. 5).

40. Andronicus, the Greek (Rom. xvi. 7).

41, 42. Titus; Timothy.

The following were with Peter in Rome:--

43, 44. Hermas; Plightâ.

45-47. Patrobas; Asyncritus; Hermas.

The following came with Peter to Cornelius:--

48, 49. Criscus (II Tim. iv. 10); Milichus.

50, 51. Kîrîtôn (Crito); Simon.

52. Gaius, who received Paul.

53, 54. Abrazon (?); Apollos.

The following were rejected from among the Seventy, for they were followers of Cerinthus, and denied our Lord's divinity:--

55-57. Simon; Levi; Bar-Kubbâ.

58-60. Cleon; Hymenaeus; Candarus.

61-63. Clithon (?); Demas; Narcissus.

64-66. Slîkîspus; Thaddaeus; Mârûthâ.

In their stead there came in:--

Luke, the Physician.

Apollos, the elect.

Ampelius; Urbanus; Stachys.

Popillius (Publius); Aristobulus.

Stephen; Herodion, the son of Narcissus.

Olympas; Mark, the Evangelist.

Addai; Aggai; Mâr Mârî.

CHRONOLOGY

From Adam to the Flood was	2262 years.
From the Flood to Abraham was	1015 "
From Abraham to the Exodus from Egypt was	430 "
From the Exodus to Solomon and the building of the Temple was	400 "
From Solomon to the First Captivity, which Nebuchadnezzar led away captive	495 "

From the First Captivity to the prophesying of Daniel was	180	"
From the prophesying of Daniel to the Birth of our Lord was	483	"
	5265	"

All these make 5345 years (*sic*).

| From Alexander to our Lord was | 303 years. |
| From our Lord to Constantine was | 341 " |

In the year 438 of Alexander, the Macedonian, the kingdom of the Persians had its beginning.

For 438 read 538, as the Sasanian dynasty was founded by Ardashîr I in A.D. 226.

Know, O my brother readers, that from the beginning of the creation of Adam to Alexander was 5180 years.

OF GOG AND MAGOG

When Alexander was king, and had subdued countries and cities, and had arrived in the East, he saw in the confines of the East those men who are of the children of Japhet. They were more wicked and unclean than all [other] dwellers in the world; filthy people of hideous appearance, who ate mice and the creeping things of the earth, and snakes and scorpions. They never buried the bodies of their dead [but ate them]. People ignorant of God, and unacquainted with the power of reason, but who lived in this world without understanding like ravening beasts. When Alexander saw their wickedness, he called God to his aid, and he gathered together and brought them and their wives and children, and made them go in, and shut them up within the confines of the North. This is the gate of the world on the north, and there is no other entrance or exit from the confines of the world from the east to the north. And Alexander prayed to God with tears, and God heard his prayer and commanded those two lofty mountains which are called "the children of the north," and they drew nigh to one another until there remained between them about twelve cubits. Then he built in front of them a strong building, and he made for it a door of brass, and anointed it within and without with oil of Thesnaktîs (i.e. an oil which cannot be burnt off with fire or scraped off with an iron tool), so that if they should bring iron implements near it to force it to open, they would be unable to move it; and if they wished to melt it with fire, it would quench it; and it feared neither the operations of devils nor of sorcerers, and was not to be overcome [by them]. Now there were twenty-two kingdoms imprisoned within the northern gate, and their names are these:--

Gôg, Mâgôg.
Nâwâl, Eshkenâz (Eshkîn).
Denâphâr (Dîfâr).
Paktâyê (the people of Paktuê in the Thracian Chersonesus).
Welôtâyê (Lûdâyê).
Humnâyê (the Huns), Parzâyê.
Daklâyê, Thaubelâyê (Tuklâyê).
Darmetâyê, Kawkebâyê.
Dog-men (Cynocephali).
Emderâthâ, Garmîdô.
Cannibals, Therkâyê (Thracians).
Âlânâyê (the Allani), Pisilôn.
Denkâyê (Dunkâyê).
Saltrâyê (Saltâyê).

At the end of the world and at the final consummation, when men are eating and drinking and marrying wives; and women are given to husbands; when they are planting vineyards and building buildings, and there is neither wicked man nor adversary, on account of the assured tranquillity and certain peace; suddenly the gates of the north shall be opened, and the hosts of the nations that are imprisoned there shall go forth. The whole earth shall tremble before them, and men shall flee and take refuge in the mountains and in caves and in burial places, and in clefts of the earth; and they shall die of hunger, and there will be none to bury them, by reason of the multitude of afflictions which they will make men suffer. They will eat dead dogs and cats; they will give mothers the bodies of their children to cook, and they will eat them before them without shame. They will destroy the earth, and there will be none able to stand before them. After one week of that sore affliction, they will all be destroyed in the plain of Joppa, for thither will all those [people] be gathered together, with their wives and their sons and their daughters.

OF THE COMING OF ANTI-CHRIST

In a week and half a week after the destruction of these wretches shall the son of destruction appear. He shall be conceived in Chorazin, born in Bethsaida, and reared in Capernaum. Chorazin shall exult because he was conceived in her, Bethsaida because he was born in her, and Capernaum because he was brought up in her; for this reason our Lord proclaimed Woe to these three [cities] in the Gospel (Matt. xi. 21). As soon as the son of perdition is revealed the king of the Greeks will go up and stand upon Golgotha, where our Lord was crucified; and he will set the royal crown upon the top of the holy Cross, upon which our Lord was crucified; and he will stretch out his two hands to heaven, and will deliver over the kingdom to God the Father. The holy Cross shall be taken up to heaven, and the royal crown with it; and the king will die immediately. The king who shall deliver over the kingdom to God will be descended from the seed of Kûshath, the daughter of Pîl, the king of the Ethiopians; for Armelaus (Romulus), the king of the Greeks, took Kûshath to wife, and the seed of the Ethiopians was mingled with that of the Greeks. From this seed shall a king arise who shall deliver the kingdom over to God, as the blessed David hath said, "Cush will deliver the power to God" (Ps. lxviii. 31).

When the Cross is raised up to heaven straightway shall every head and every ruler and all powers be brought to nought, and God will withdraw His providential care from the earth. The heavens will be prevented from letting fall rain, and the earth from producing germs and plants; and the earth shall remain like iron through drought, and the heavens like brass. Then will the son of perdition appear, of the seed and of the tribe of Dan; and he will show deluding phantasms, and lead astray the world, for the simple will see the lepers cleansed, the blind with their eyes opened, the paralytic walking, the devils cast out, the sun when he looks upon it becoming black, the moon when he commands it becoming changed, the trees putting forth fruit from their branches, and the earth making roots to grow. He will show deluding phantasms [of this kind], but he will not be able to raise the dead. He will go into Jerusalem and will sit upon a throne in the Temple, saying, "I am the Christ," and he will be borne aloft by legions of devils like a king and a lawgiver, naming himself God, and saying, "I am the fulfilment of the types and the parables." He will put an end to prayers and offerings, as if at his appearance prayers are to be abolished and men will not need sacrifices and offerings along with him. He becomes a man incarnate by a married woman of the tribe of Dan. When this son of destruction becomes a man, he will be made a dwelling place for devils, and all Satanic workings will be perfected in him. There will be gathered together with him all the devils and all the hosts of the Indians; and before all the Indians and before all men will the mad Jewish nation believe in him, saying, "This is the Christ, the expectation of the world." The time of the error of the Anti-christ will last two years and a half, but others say three years and six months. And when everyone is standing in despair, then will Elijah (Elias) come from Paradise, and convict the deceiver, and turn the heart of the fathers to the children and the heart of the children to the fathers; and he will encourage and strengthen the hearts of the believers.

THE HEBREW BIBLE TRANSLATED INTO GREEK

Ptolemy Philadelphus reigned 38 years. In the third (or, sixth) year of his reign the fifth millennium from the creation of the world ended. This king asked the Jews who were captives in Egypt, and seventy (or, seventy-two) old men translated the Scriptures for him, from Hebrew into Greek, in the Island of Pharos. In return for this he set them free, and gave back to them also the ves sels of their temple. Their names were:--

1.	Josephus Hezekiah Zechariah John Ezekiel Elisha	Of the tribe of Reuben.
2.	Judah Simon Samuel Addai Mattathias Shalmi	Of the tribe of Simeon.
3.	Nehemiah Joseph Theodosius Bâsâ Adonijah Dâkî	Of the tribe of Levi.
4.	Jothan Abdî Elisha Ananias	Of the tribe of Judah.

	Zechariah	
	Hilkiah	
5.	Isaac	Of the tribe of Issachar.
	Jacob	
	Jesus	
	Sambât	
	(Sabbateus)	
	Simon	
	Levi	
6.	Judah	Of the tribe of Zebulon.
	Joseph	
	Simon	
	Zechariah	
	Samuel	
	Shamlî	
7.	Sambât	Of the tribe of Gad.
	Zedekiah	
	Jacob	
	Isaac	
	Jesse	
	Matthias	
8.	Theodosius	Of the tribe of Asher.
	Jason	
	Joshua	
	John	
	Theodotus	
	Jothan	

9.	Abraham	Of the tribe of Dan.
	Theophilus	
	Arsam	
	Jason	
	Jeremiah	
	Daniel	
10.	Jeremiah	Of the tribe of Naphtali.
	Eliezer	
	Zechariah	
	Benaiah	
	Elisha	

	Dathî	
11.	Samuel Josephus Judah Jonathan Dositheus Caleb	Of the tribe of Joseph.
12.	Isalus John Theodosius Arsam Abijah Ezekiel	Of the tribe of Benjamin

Ptolemy II, surnamed Philadelphus, was the son of Ptolemy I, Soter, by Beremce, and was born 308 B.C.; he reigned as sole king from 283 to 247 B.C., when he died. His name was transcribed by the Egyptian annalists thus:--

PTU[O]LMIS

and his title Philadelphus by   I *meri sen* (*i.e.* "brother-loving"). He enlarged the great Alexandrian Library, which was founded by his father, and in his day it is said to have contained as many as 400,000 books, (*i.e.* rolls of papyrus). It was by his orders that Manetho, a priest of Sebennytus in the Delta compiled his History of Egypt.

ABRAHAM AND THE CITY OF UR

THE paragraphs which the author of the "Cave Treasures" devotes to the history of Terah and Abraham throw new light upon the lives of these patriarchs and the conditions under which they lived in the city of Ur, and they contain many interesting details which are not recorded in the Book of Genesis, and some new information concerning the overthrow of the city of Ur by the "Wind Flood." It is quite clear that Terah and Abraham were great, powerful and wealthy shêkhs, and their large flocks of sheep and goats and herds of camels suggest that they were owners and breeders of cattle on a large scale, and masters of caravans. The three hundred and eighteen trained men, born in his house (Gen. xiv. 14), whom Abraham armed and sent forth to rescue Lot, his nephew, were probably the armed guards who marched with his flocks and herds and caravans and protected them. Up to the present no person mentioned in the cuneiform inscriptions can be identified either with Terah or Abraham, but all the facts which the recent excavations at Ur have brought to light show that in Abraham's day the inhabitants of the city were given up wholly to idolatry, their chief object of worship being Nannar, the Moon-god. Not only did Abraham smash his father's idols, but under the divine guidance he freed himself from the custom of offering up his firstborn to devils. Further, when he saw his city attacked by hosts of enemies from the north and from the low-lying lands to the south, there was nothing left for him to do but migrate to the country which God promised to give him. Putting all the evidence together, it is clear that Abraham was a great, strong and independent chief in Babylonia, and that his power waxed greater when he established himself at Harrân. The rescue of Lot shows that his armed retainers formed an effective military body, and the greatness of his might and influence is proved by the fact that he compelled Ephron the Hittite to sell him the cave of Machpelah. And the Pharaoh, king of Egypt, who seized Sarah, would hardly have listened to Abraham's objections unless he knew that Abraham had a following strong enough to make his restitution of Sarah a necessity.

THE EXCAVATIONS AT UR OF THE CHALDEES

Of the greatness and importance of Ur of the Chaldees politically and commercially, the excavations which Mr. C. L. Woolley has conducted for the British Museum and the University of Pennsylvania during the last five years afford abundant evidence. In my little book, Babylonian Life and History, London, 1925, I gave a brief summary of what had been done up to the time of going to press, and it is necessary to describe the progress of the work during the winters of 1924-25 and 1925-26. The facts are derived from Mr. Woolley's official reports, published in the Antiquaries' Journal, Vol. V, No. 4, and Vol. VI, No. 4. As already said, the Ziggurat which stands in the west corner of the Temenos enclosure was cleared during the winter of 1923-24, and in 1924-25 work was begun on the Temenos or Sacred Area itself. A good general view of the site already excavated is given on Plate III. Already in 1925, Mr. Woolley was able to report as follows: "Summarizing our results in this part of the field, we can say that we have now a complete plan of the Ziggurat and its surroundings in the Neo-Babylonian period after the wholesale reconstructions of Nebuchadnezzar II and Nabonidus, the complete plan of the Kassite period for three sides of the Ziggurat, a good part of the plan of the buildings of the Larsa period (2000 B.C.), and that of Ur-Engur's (i.e. Ur-Nammu's) work on one side of the tower, together with a general idea of its lines on two of the other sides." The Ziggurat of Ur-Nammu was built on a terrace which on this side had a width of 34 metres, and cones of baked clay bearing Ur-Nammu's dedication of the building E-temen-ni-il had been inserted in the vertical joints of the brickwork. For the first time these cones were found in their original position. A specimen of these cones is given on Plate IV. Ur-Nammu built E Nannar, or Temple of the Moon-god, on the terrace level of E-temen-ni-il. During the Larsa period Ur-Nammu's buildings were reconstructed, and prominent among the kings who carried out this work were Sinidinnam (2086-2080 B.C.) and Warad Sin (2072-2060 B.C.). Cones and other monuments show that En-an-na-tum, high-priest of Nannar, and son of king Ishme-Dagan, and Sumu-ilum, who built a temple to Innina, and Silli-Adad, and Kudur Mabug had all worked here.

The principal builder at Ur during the Kassite period was Kuri-Galzu, but his work was not of the best kind, and as his successors did no repairs on his buildings, they fell into decay. The arched doorway which he built in the sanctuary of E-Dublal-maḫ is shown on Plate IV. For seven hundred years nothing of importance in connection with the temple buildings at Ur was done. Nebuchadnezzar II and his grandson practically rebuilt the public buildings at Ur. They found the ancient shrines so hopelessly destroyed or so completely buried that on a traditional site they were able to employ a new design or radically to reshape the old, and even to change the location of a sanctuary whose name alone perhaps survived. Under the rule of the Persians the city gradually sunk into ruin and decay.

To the south-east of the Ziggurat stood the Temple of Nin-gal, which was built by Sinbalatsu-ikbi (see the door socket of this king on Plate VIII), the Assyrian governor of Ur (650 B.C.), and was restored by Nabonidus. Mr. Woolley's excavations showed that it was built on the site of the first temple of Nin-gal, which dated from the reign of Kuri-Galzu in the XIVth century B.C.

To the south-east of the temple E-Nun-Mah are the temple E-Dublal-Mah, the work of Kuri-Galzu (Plate V), and the E-Gig-Par which was built by Nabonidus (Plate VI). The latter building is 95 metres long and 50 metres wide, and is oriented N.W. and S.E., and there is no doubt that it was the convent in which Bêl-Shalti-Nannar, daughter of Nabonidus and sister of Belshazzar, ruled as Lady Superior of the sacred women of Ur. In the rooms of this convent were found a very large number of small but important objects, e.g. gate sockets, sculptured reliefs, school-exercise tablets, teaching tablets, tablets marked with squares in lines used in playing games, etc., and one room was used as a Museum, for it contained inscribed objects with labels attached for teaching purposes! The remains found in E-Dublal-Mah included portions of a statue, dating from 2800 B.C.; a limestone plaque with reliefs representing the worship of Nannar (Plate XIII, No. 1); portions of the great stele of Ur-Nammu (Plate XI, No. 2); alabaster rams forming the sides of a throne (Plate XIII, No. 2); etc.

During the winter of 1925-26, Mr. Woolley and his men excavated the great Gig-Par-ku site at Ur. The earliest buildings of which any actual ruins were found belonged to the period of the First Dynasty of Ur (about 4000-3500 B.C.). In digging down to trace the Third Dynasty foundations, they found a short section of a wall constructed with kiln-burnt plano-convex bricks set over a foundation of rough limestone blocks, a wall identical in every respect with that of the temple built by king A-an-nî-pad-da at Al-`Ubêd. Among the buildings of the Third Dynasty of Ur (2300 B.C.) was the temple of Ur-Nammu, but remains of its walls are wanting. Thirteen gate sockets were found, and the inscription on them reads, "Ur-Nammu, the mighty man, the king of Ur, the king of Sumer and Akkad, has built the splendid Gig-Par for his Lady Nin-Gal" (Plate VII, Nos. 2 and 3). On the ruins of Ur-Nammu's temple his grandson Bur-Sin built a temple which was dedicated by him to the goddess Nin-Gal. An inscribed door socket of Bur-Sin is shown on Plate VIII. This temple was probably destroyed about 2000 B.C. by the Elamites, who captured the city and brought the rule of the Third Dynasty of Ur to an end.

The next temple that occupied the site was built by En-an-na-tum, son of Ishme-Dagan, king of Isin. The building was rectangular and measured 79 metres by 76½ metres, and its angles were oriented to the cardinal points of the compass. It was surrounded by a massive wall, and had two entrances; at the east angle was a gate tower. The building was divided into three parts by the cross corridor, and by a wall running parallel with it; it contained two temples, several small shrines, and a considerable number of small rooms, in which the priests and priestesses lived. Some of the rooms were used as kitchens and pantries, and some as sepulchral chambers in which the bodies of dead priests were buried. A view of the great kitchen in Gig Par Ku is given on Plate IX. The building supplies a complete plan of an early Sumerian sanctuary, which has hitherto been wanting. The temple flourished in a greater or lesser degree all through the reign of Hammurabi, and down to the eleventh year of the reign of his son Samsu-iluna; its destruction probably took place during, or as a result of, the revolt which took place in the following year. Among the important objects found in the ruins may be mentioned:--1. A diorite statuette of the goddess Eau, the great "World- Mother" (Plate X), which was made about 2400 B.C. 2. Diorite statuette of the goddess Nin-Gal (about 2080 B.C.). 3. A limestone plaque on which are sculptured scenes of worship (about 3000 B.C.) (Plate XI, No. 1). 4. An alabaster model of the lunar disk dedicated to Nannar by the daughter of Sargon of Agade (about 2630 B.C.). 5. A granite bowl of Naram-Sin of Agade (2550 B.C.), which about 300 years later (about 2250 B.C.) was presented to the temple at Ur by the daughter of king Dungi (or, Shulgi).

The excavation of the "Palace Site "has yielded much useful information, and the further exploration of the so-called Tomb Mound has laid bare the foundations of many houses, and yielded many small, but interesting, antiquities, tablets, terra-cotta figures, cylinder seals, pottery, etc. Among the tablets were several dating from the period of Rim-Sin (1980 B.C.); these were inscribed with hymns and religious texts written in honour of the Moon-god Nannar.

Mr. C. L. Woolley resurned work at Ur on October 28, 1926, and continued the excavations until February, 1927, when want of funds brought his operations to a standstill. The results of his labours during the past winter are of extraordinary importance, and through the courtesy of Sir Frederic Kenyon, Director of the British Museum, and the late Dr. Byron Gordon, Director of the Museum of the University of Pennsylvania at Philadelphia, I am enabled to describe them briefly in the following pages.

The site first selected for work during the past winter was a lofty mound outside the wall built by Nebuchadnezzar II round the Sacred Area, and when a space measuring 200 feet by 150 feet was cleared, several blocks of houses, divided by narrow streets, were found. Hitherto the Expedition had excavated only temples and fortifications which, after all, tell us little or nothing about the private daily life of Abraham's neighbours, but Mr. Woolley felt that the time had come for him to explore the ruins of the houses of the merchants and the poorer class of inhabitants of "Ur of the Chaldees," and the results he obtained greatly exceeded his expectations. When a house fell down in Babylonia the ruins were levelled and another house was built on them, and in some mounds several layers of houses, each layer belonging to a different period, have been identified. On the site selected by Mr. Woolley the rains and winds and storms of four thousand years had removed all the more modern layers of houses, and he was able to get to work at once on a fine collection of houses which were built about 2100 B.C. The main walls being built of burnt brick, were in a good state of preservation; the interior walls were of mud brick, laid on burnt brick foundations, which rose two or three feet above the brick-paved floor. Thus the foundations formed a "damp course," and the state of the walls showed that the dwellers in the houses were not troubled by damp. The visitor, on passing through the doorway, entered a small ante-chamber, which led into the courtyard; this was partly covered in. The reception room was on one side, and the kitchen and pantry, etc., were on the other. The bedrooms of the family were on the upper floor, which were entered from a wooden gallery running round all four sides of the court yard. Close to the front door was the stairway, the treads of which are made of solid brick. The walls of these houses are still about 20 feet in height, and the plan of them and the general arrangement of the rooms on the ground floor and upper floor are reproduced to this day in the houses of merchants and well-to-do folk at Baghdâd and Hillah. There is little doubt that it was in houses of this kind that Serug, Terah, Nahor and Abraham lived. The houses and their courtyards stood side by side in rows, as at the present day; the streets then as now were narrow. An excellent representation of a street is given on Plate XII. {See page 283 for a drawing of the interior of a private house.}

When the master of the house died he was usually buried under it, together with his engraved stone cylinder-seal, pots, and inscribed clay tablets. As was to be expected, no furniture of any shape or kind was found in the houses, and even the burial places under them had been rifled. But, in spite of this, Mr. Woolley succeeded in collecting from the site a considerable number of clay tablets inscribed with tables of square and cube roots, hymns, and records of the buildings erected by various kings of Ur. Among the miscellaneous objects found may be mentioned a bottle of blue and black glass which probably came from Syria; this interesting object was probably made about 1500 B.C..

The works that were carried out after the excavation of the houses was finished threw much light upon the history of Ur in the first half of the third minennium B.C. There is now no doubt that a temple tower or Ziggurat existed at Ur as early as 2800 B.C., for portions of its walls made of plano-convex mud bricks were found buried under the Ziggurat made by Ur-Nammu 2600 B.C. Under the temple of E-nin-makh a very interesting object was discovered in the shape of the cover of an ivory toilet box bearing a Phoenician inscription (see Plate XIV, No. 1), and with it were several articles for the toilet in ivory, and a beautifully engraved comb. The remains of the royal buildings, which were erected about 2000 B.C., prove that the Sumerians, even at that early period, were able to construct halls with arches and vaulted roofs. It is clear that many of the statements which were made by architectural authorities two or three generations ago will have to be greatly modified in the light of the discoveries made at Ur. In a great commercial centre like Ur accurate weights were of prime importance, and the fine diorite duck-weight inscribed with the name of king Shulgi shows that as early as 2500 B.C. standard weights were in use in Babylonia (see Plate VII, No. 1). This standard was in use in Babylonia two thousand years later, as an inscription on a weight of Nebuchadnezzar II testifies.

The next portion of the site selected for careful excavation was the area at the south-east end, inside the wall built by Nebuchadnezzar II, where there were no buildings. A trench cut across it brought to light an early cemetery, containing graves which were made not much later than 3000 B.C. These graves yielded a large quantity of pottery; vases in diorite, hard stone, alabaster, and steatite, many of beautiful shape and design; copper bowls, vases, pots, axe-heads, adzes, spears, razors, knives and daggers; gold, silver and carnelian beads; lapis lazuli pins with heads of gold or silver; cylinder-seals beautifully engraved; rock-crystal cylinder-seals with copper caps and cores made of white or coloured paste; gold tiaras, chains, finger-rings, ear-rings, beads, amulets, etc. All these show that the crafts of the metal worker and the jeweller had reached a very high state of perfection when the first kings of the Ist dynasty of Ur began to reign in the second half of the fourth millennium B.C. When these graves were made they were only about one foot below the level of the surrounding country, but now they lie some 15 or 20 feet under the accumulated rubbish of fifty centuries. The latest graves were, according to Mr. Woolley, made about 3000 B.C., and the earliest some 500 years earlier. Among the objects found in the lowermost layer of graves were two cylinder-seals each inscribed with the name of a king of Ur who reigned over the city several hundreds of years before its history as a great commercial centre began. In the uppermost layer the cylinder-seals are inscribed with the names of officers of the household of the daughter of Sargon of Agade, about 2600 B.C. This princess was the High Priestess of the Moon-god of Ur.

The four principal methods of burial were as follows:--(1) The body, in its ordinary apparel, was wrapped in a mat and laid on a mat at the bottom of the grave; the vases, weapons, ornaments, etc., were placed round about it. (2) The body was placed in a wickerwork coffin, together with the small objects; the vessels in pottery, stone, etc., were grouped round it. (3) The body was laid in a wooden coffin, with the objects to be buried with it, some being enclosed in little coffers. (4) The body was laid in an oval case made of clay. In the oldest graves of all, traces of partial cremation were found. The problem of how the early Sumerians disposed of their dead has now been solved. As the Egyptians buried their dead on the west bank of the Nile, so also did the Sumerians transport the bodies of their dead across the great canal which flowed by the west wall of the city of Ur, and bury them in the western desert.

Before the close of the season cylinder-seals bearing the names of five early kings, of whom three were unknown to history, were found. From the lapis lazuli cylinder-seal of Queen Nin-Kur-Nin the name of her husband Mes-anni-padda   , the founder of the Ist dynasty of

Ur has been recovered. Several of the kings of this dynasty have hitherto been regarded as mythical.

Below the black stratum which lies under the graves of the period of 3000 B.C. the richest graves were found. Here were discovered clay tablets, inscribed with a semi-pictographic script, and seals bearing the names of kings unrecorded in history. Among the other important "finds" may be mentioned:--(1) Eight shell plaques decorated with linear patterns (see Plate XV) and animal figures; the lines are filled in with colour, red and black. (2) A royal gaming board, which consists of 20 shell plaques, decorated with linear designs and inlay of red paste and lapis lazuli, and framed with lapis lazuli, ivory and mother-of-pearl. It is the Sumerian equivalent of the so-called draught-boards which have been found in Egyptian tombs, and seems to indicate that the Sumerians, as well as the Egyptians, believed that their dead amused themselves by playing some game like that of draughts in the Other World.

But the greatest "find" of all was made just before the end of the season. About 18 feet below the level of the ground Mr. Woolley came upon a hoard of copper tools and weapons. This consisted of sets of chisels and bundles of heavy spear-heads, and side by side with these were two gold chisels and a gold spear-head. Further research brought to light more copper weapons, arrows by the quiverful, lance-points, a mace, axe-heads, and parts of bows. Round about these were pendants in carnelian, lapis lazuli and gold, the gold binding for a bow, an adze of solid gold, its wooden handle being covered with plaster painted red and bound with thin gold. Lying a little apart was a silver baldric, to which was attached a "vanity case" of gold filigree work, containing a pair of tiny tweezers, spoon and stiletto, all of gold, hung upon a silver ring. Close by was a dagger (see Plate XIV, No. 2). The hilt is formed of one piece of deep-coloured lapis lazuli studded with gold, and the blade is of burnished gold; the sheath is of solid gold. The back of the latter is plain except for two lines of simple beading, but the front is entirely covered with an intricate design in filigree work. The dagger and its sheath are marvels of design and workmanship, and as they were made at least fifty-five centuries ago, they are among the oldest and finest specimens of the craft of the goldsmith in the world.

All the more important antiquities which have fallen to the share of the Trustees of the British Museum are exhibited in the Babylonian Rooms of the Museum, and are on view all day and every day. Mr. Woolley has written and published in October each year in The Antiquaries' Journal a detailed report, with excellent plans and a large number of photographic plates, of the work done at Ur during the preceding winter, and to these the reader who requires fuller and more detailed information about the work is begged to refer. The Trustees of the British Museum have also decided to publish a full scientific Report on the work, with maps, plans, and photographs, and the first volume of it, which deals with the discovery of the temple of A-an-ni-pad-da at Tall al-ʿUbêd, near Ur, by Dr. H. R. Hall, and the completion of its excavation by Mr. Woolley, has already appeared. A smaller work on the temple of Tall al-ʿUbêd is being prepared by Dr. H. R. Hall, and Mr. C. J. Gadd, of the British Museum, is writing the history of Ur from the time of the Seven Wise Men who flourished before the Flood to the final downfall and decay of the city about 300 B.C.

BIBLIOGRAPHY

BARTHOLOMEW, THE APOSTLE. Book of the Resurrection of Christ (in Budge, Coptic Apocrypha, London, 1913).

BASSET, RENÉ. Les Prières de la Vierge à Bartos et au Golgotha, Paris, 1895. French translation from the Ethiopic.

BEZOLD, C. Die Schatzhöhle. Syriac text, Leipzig, 1883; German translation, Leipzig, 1888.

BUDGE, E. A. WALLIS. The Contendings of the Apostles. Ethiopic texts and English translations, 2 vols., London, 1889-1901.
    Book of the Bee. Syriac text and English translations, Oxford, 1886.
    The History of the Blessed Virgin Mary, and the History of the Likeness of Christ which the Jews of Tiberias made to mock at. Syriac and English, 2 vols., London, 1899-1901.
    Legends of our Lady Mary. Translations from the Ethiopic, London, 1922.

BUDGE, E. A. WALLIS. Coptic Apocrypha. Coptic and English, London, 1913.
    Miscellaneous Coptic texts. Coptic and English, London, 1915.

CHARLES, CANON R. H. The Book of Enoch, translated from Dillmann's Ethiopic text, Oxford, 1893.

DILLMANN, A. Liber Henoch Aethiopice, Leipzig, 1851.
    Das Buch Henosh übersetzt und erklärt, Leipzig, 1853.

ENGER, M. Joannis Apostoli de Transitu Beatae Mariae Virginis Liber, Elberfeld, 1854.

FABRICIUS, J. A. Codex Apocryphus Novi Testamenti, 3 vols., Hamburg, 1719-43.

HOFFMANN, A. G. Das Buch Henoch in vollständiger Übersetzung, 2 vols., Jena, 1833-38.

LAWRENCE, R. The Book of Enoch the Prophet, Oxford, 1838, English translation.

JAMES, M; R. The Apocryphal New Testament, Oxford, 1924. This comprehensive work entirely supersedes Hone's Apocryphal New Testament.
  Apocrypha Anecdota, I, Cambridge, 1893.

LEWIS, A. S. Mythological Acts of the Apostles, Cambridge, 1904 (in Arabic).

LIPSIUS, R. A. Die apokryphen Apostelgeshichten, Brunswick, 1883-90.

LIPSIUS, R. A., and BONNET, M. Acta Apostolorum, Leipzig, 1891-1903.

MALAN, S. C. The Book of Adam and Eve, or the Conflict of Adam with Satan, London, 1822. Translation from the Ethiopic.

PHILLIPS, G. The Doctrine of Addai, the Apostle, London, 1876.

ROBINSON, F. Coptic Apocryphal Gospels, Cambridge, 1896.

THILO, J. C. Codex Apocryphus Novi Testamenti, Leipzig, 1832.

TISCHENDORF, C. Apocalypses Apocryphae, Leipzig, 1866.

TRUMPP, E. Gadla Adam, Der Kampf Adams gegen die Versuchungen des Satans. Das christliche Adambuch des Morgenlandes, Munich, 1880. Ethiopic text.
  Die Hexaëmeron des Pseudo-Epiphanius, Munich, 1882. Ethiopic text and German translation.

WRIGHT, W. "Contributions to the Apocryphal Literature of the New Testament" (in Journal of Sacred Literature, Vol. VI, pp. 417-448, and Vol. VII, pp. 110-160, January and April, 1865).
  Apocryphal Acts of the Apostles, 2 vols., 1871.

ENDNOTES

---

[1] The Copts have a remarkable legend about the origin of wheat. According to this, our Lord commanded the Cherubim to take John the disciple and show him the mysteries of heaven and earth. Whilst they were journeying together through the heavens, John asked his guide to tell him the history of the wheat plant and where it was first found. The angel said that after Adam and Eve were driven forth from Paradise they were banished to Havilah (Gen. ii. 11), "Where they suffered greatly because they could not eat the poor food which the country produced. The pangs of hunger vexed them sorely, and at length they cried out to God and told Him that they were starving. Our Lord, the Word, had pity upon them, and said to His Father, "Behold, the man whom we have created in Our image and likeness is an hungered; now, if it be Thy will, do not let him die before Thy face." In reply God said to Him, "If Thou art moved with compassion for the man whom We have created, and who hath rejected My commandment, go Thou and give him Thine own flesh and let him eat thereof, for it is Thou Who hast made Thyself his advocate." Then our Lord took a little piece of the flesh of His divine side, and rubbed it down into small pieces, and showed them to His Father. When God saw them He said to His Son, "Wait, and I will give Thee some of My own flesh, which is invisible." Then God took a portion of His own body, and made it into a grain of wheat, and He sealed the grain in the middle with the seal wherewith He sealed the worlds of light, and then gave it to our Lord and told Him to give it to Michael, the archangel, who was to give it to Adam and teach him how to sow and reap it. Michael found Adam by the Jordan, who as he had eaten nothing for eight days was crying to God for food, and as soon as Adam received the grain of wheat, he ceased to cry out, and became strong, and his descendants have lived on wheat ever since. Water, wheat and the throne of God "are the equals of the Son of God." See Brit. Mus. MS. Oriental No. 7026, Fol. 5aff (ed. Budge, Coptic Apocrypha, p. 244). (p. 10)

[2] "And Abgar wished himself to pass over and go to Palestine, and see with his own eyes all which Christ was doing; but because he was not able to pass through the country of the Romans, which was not his, lest this cause should call forth bitter enmity, he wrote a letter and sent it to Christ by the hand of Hannan, the keeper of the archives."--Phillips, The Doctrine of Addai, London, 1876, page 3. (p. 12)

[3] See Kebra Nagast (Budge's translation), chapter c. Concerning the Angels who rebelled. (p. 45)

This is the order in which this paragraph appears in the text, though in the "Genealogy of our Lord" (see below, page 233) the circumcision and the presentation in the Temple precede the flight into Egypt. (p. 113)

[5] I.e. five thousand five hundred years. (p. 128)

www.ingramcontent.com/pod-product-compliance
Lightning Source LLC
Chambersburg PA
CBHW050842270326
41930CB00019B/3432